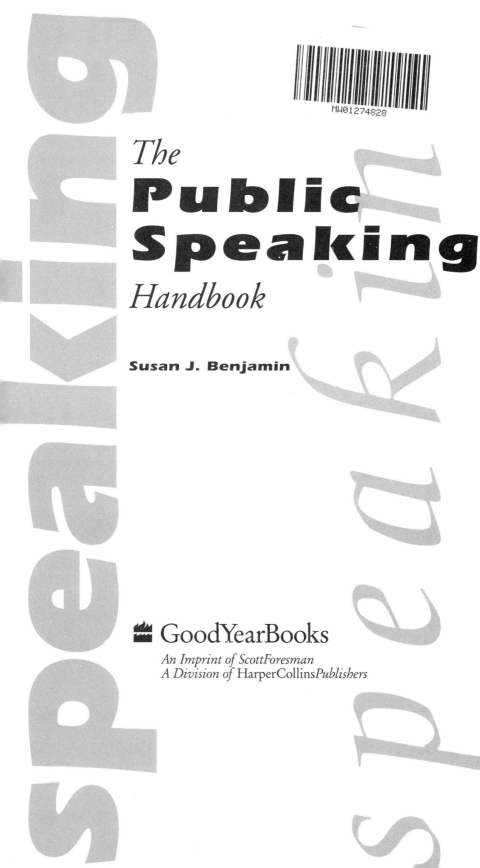

The
Public
Speaking
Handbook

Susan J. Benjamin

GoodYearBooks

An Imprint of ScottForesman
A Division of HarperCollins*Publishers*

Dedication
This book is dedicated to the students and teachers of
Highland Park and Deerfield High Schools who sharpen
their communication skills every day.

Acknowledgments
English/Speech teachers Ruth Freer and Erin Mack deserve
special acknowledgement for sharing their own and their students' excellent work for parts of this book. Students past and
present, Richenda Frankel, Scott Green, Taka Ichinose, Peter
Kupfer, Rachel Rosenbaum, Steve Ruken, Adam Saffro, Bram
Spector and Debbie Widman receive a special note of gratitude
for the fine quality of their work as displayed in the classroom
and in these pages.

GoodYearBooks are available for most basic curriculum subjects
plus many enrichment areas. For more GoodYearBooks, contact
your local bookseller or educational dealer. For a complete catalog with information about other GoodYearBooks, please write:

GoodYearBooks
ScottForesman
1900 East Lake Avenue
Glenview, IL 60025

Book design by Karen Kohn and Associates.

ISBN 0-673-36159-4

1 2 3 4 5 6 7 8 9 - DQ - 04 03 02 01 00 99 98 97 96

TABLE OF CONTENTS

INTRODUCTION

Some years ago, authors David Wallechinsky, Irving Wallace, and Amy Wallace presented a series of lists in their best-selling book *The Book of Lists.* One of the lists, compiled by a team of market researchers, was entitled "The 14 Worst Human Fears." After asking three thousand Americans, "What is your greatest fear?", 41 percent replied, "Speaking before a group." The fear of public speaking topped the list of fourteen as the worst human fear (Wallechinsky, 469).

Why did this fear rank above such typically fear-arousing situations as heights, deep water, sickness, or death? One explanation might be that our egos, our sense of ourselves, are important to us, and when we speak publicly we put our egos on the line. We all want to present ourselves in the best light possible. We want to be liked and accepted by others; we also want to earn their respect.

When we are put in a position of speaking in front of others, particularly to a large group, we are putting ourselves on display. Audience members can judge the quality of our message, as well as our personal characteristics. Putting ourselves on center stage makes us nervous because we want to do a good job and win the approval of others.

Most of us will give speeches at some point in our lives. The fact that you are reading this page indicates that you are probably getting ready to give a speech. The best way to deal with the normal anxiety that accompanies public speaking is to prepare the speech carefully. Preparing the speech means that you know ahead of time what you will say and how you plan to present content. The information should be organized so that listeners can follow the pattern of your thoughts, and the content should be specific and new to your audience. The final part of speech preparation involves delivery: you should plan to present information in an interesting, attention-sustaining manner.

In the following chapters, you will learn about the theory and practice of effective speaking. The chapters will also take you through the steps necessary for preparing and delivering an excellent speech. If you follow these steps, you may still experience the normal pre-performance jitters, but you will conquer what *The Book of Lists* terms the "number-one worst human fear." You will also learn how to communicate in a manner that will please and enlighten others.

1

THE SPEECH CHAIN: FOSTERING REAL COMMUNICATION

Why do we give speeches? We speak primarily to share information with others. The speaker sends out a message to begin the process. Listeners receive it and send back a message. The message the listener sends back to the speaker is called *feedback*. After receiving the feedback, the speaker sends out new messages, and the communication cycle continues. Giving a speech is truly a circular process, as indicated in the Speech Chain below (Jerowski, et al, 12).

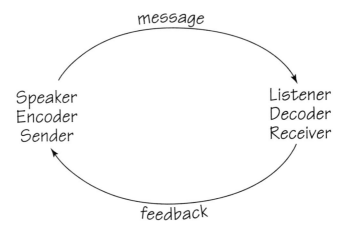

The Speech Chain illustrates *the process of real communication,* the goal of every speaker. In real communication, messages flow back and forth; the speaker is not talking merely to take up sound space. When you are speaking, how can you make sure that real communication will happen? First, the content of your speech should be well-prepared and engaging. How to gather and organize content can be found in Chapters 2 and 3. Then, as you speak, establish eye contact with as many individuals as possible. When audience members see that you are looking directly at them, they will know that you are communicating with them. While speaking, look at individuals' faces and hold each one's gaze for a few seconds. Try to get audience members to look directly into your eyes.

Well-intentioned advisors sometimes counsel nervous, novice speakers to pick out a spot on the wall beyond audience members' faces, and stare at it to avoid being distracted. Wrong! This technique may be acceptable for talking without trying to make human contact, but not for effective speaking. Other advice sometimes given to "quiet" a speaker's fears is to imagine that the audience is naked! Wrong again! Both of these suggestions detract from the real purpose of public speaking: to communicate a message. As the Speech Chain indicates, good speaking—real communication—is a constant, two-way process. In front of an audience, the speaker should concentrate solely on specific aspects of the message. The best way for you to know if or how you are communicating is to look directly at your listeners and search for feedback.

Indeed, audience members' responses to the speaker's message are every bit as important as the speaker's presentation. Feedback during the speech tells the speaker how the message is being received. Feedback may be either positive or negative. Positive feedback includes such behaviors as head nodding to indicate understanding or agreement, smiling, or raising a hand to ask a question. Negative feedback includes such behaviors as talking with others in the audience during the speech or conducting personal business, such as homework for another class.

Feedback can also indicate whether a speaker should continue or adjust his or her message. For example, if audience members start to yawn, look at the clock or place their heads on their desks, the feedback is telling you to change the way in which you are presenting the message. Adjusting your speaking rate, pausing or asking a startling question may spark the communication.

LISTENING: AN IMPORTANT LINK IN THE SPEECH CHAIN

No matter how many speeches you give, you will spend much more time listening to others than speaking yourself. For example, in a speech class, you may listen to twenty-five speeches by your fellow students for every one speech that you give. Some communication experts assert that students spend up to sixty percent of their time listening. (McCutcheon, 53) Therefore, to get the most out of what you hear, you need to develop good listening skills.

Sometimes during a class when a fellow student or teacher is speaking, tired (or even bored) students will put their heads down on their desks. The teacher may insist, "Get your heads off the desks and listen!" to which a student may reply, "I can listen with my head down." Wrong! The student is confusing *hearing*, which can be done without effort, with *listening*. Hearing is a natural, involuntary act; if your ears and auditory canals are in good working order, you can hear. We may hear noises, such as those that wake us up in the middle of the night, even when we don't want to pay attention to them. Hearing is not a matter of choice. However, to get information from a speech, real listening takes work. The listener must pay careful attention to the speaker to catch both the obvious and subtle points of the message. Thoughtful attention to the speaker's manner will reveal any hidden messages. Listening is an important skill to develop because the good listener not only acquires information being communicated, but also through his or her obvious attention, helps the speaker to do a better job of maintaining the communication cycle.

The acronym SPACE (with appreciation to educational consultants Art Costa, Marian Liebowitz and Benna Kallick) will help to illustrate some of the major points of good listening. Each letter signifies an important listening element.

S staying **silent** and waiting your turn. Good listeners never interrupt a speech in progress. Staying silent and waiting until the speaker is ready to receive questions or verbal feedback are important behaviors for listeners to remember to show respect for the speaker and to concentrate on his or her message.

P **paraphrasing**, or rephrasing the speaker's message into your own words. If, during a speech, you take advantage of your ability to think faster than someone else can talk, through paraphrasing you can give the message sense and make it your own.

A **attending**, listening actively. Real listening takes effort and attention. As you listen to a speech, you may organize it in your mind and relate the message to other pieces of knowledge. Taking notes and jotting down the main points can also help you to remember elements of the speech.

C   **critique giving**, While listening to a speech, think about ways in which to help the speaker improve his or her next performance by providing constructive feedback in the form of written or oral critiques about either the content or delivery of the speech. The speaker may be able to use these suggestions in an upcoming presentation.

E   **empathizing**, the act of feeling with someone else. Put yourself in the speaker's shoes or situation and try to empathize with the speaker or with part of the message being presented. An empathic response (feeling with someone) differs from a sympathetic response (feeling for someone) because when people are feeling with each other their thoughts and feelings are close to one another, and they may respond to each other with increased sensitivity.

Because listening is a crucial link in the Speech Chain, we need to work hard at listening skills to be strong communicators. If we concentrate on the behaviors represented by SPACE, our listening should help to complete the Speech

Chain. Listening is an internal activity; if we maximize our listening time by concentrating hard on
the message, we will become better listeners and
more attentive, positive audience members.

FEEDBACK: COMPLETING THE COMMUNICATION CYCLE

Feedback can be given at the end of a
speech. At that time,listeners may have the
opportunity to give the speaker some specific,
verbal feedback about aspects of the speech.
The way in which the criticism is presented and
the way in which criticism is received are two
important parts of the communication process.
If you deliver criticism in a positive manner, you
can help the speaker to understand and incorporate your suggestions. To be helpful, criticism
should be specific and should start and end with
"bookends" of praise. Beginning with a positive
comment will diffuse the speaker's defenses
and allow him or her to hear suggestions for improvement. The suggestions should be concrete
ideas or techniques for how a speaker might organize and/or present more effective messages in

the future. For example, imagine that Amy has just finished giving a speech. A listener/critique-giver, John, who has enjoyed Amy's speech and wants her to have a feeling of accomplishment, says, "Amy's speech was good, but she walked too much." How does John's feedback help Amy to improve the content or delivery of her next speech? Because we don't know what "good" means, John needs to explain, in specific terms, how or why the speech was good. John has preceded a criticism with a positive comment and joined the two comments with the conjunction "but." The use of this word to connect positive and critical messages negates the impact of the positive message. Amy will most likely focus on the message she hears after the "but" and forget about the praise. Therefore, to maintain the impact of the positive message, the praise and suggestions for improvement should be connected with the conjunction "and." Using "and" to connect the two comments gives them equal weight, and will not make the speaker feel "put down" or defensive.

Post-speech feedback is most effective when presented directly to the speaker. Being talked *to* is much better than being talked *about*.

Therefore, if John combines specific comments with direct address, he might say, "Amy, I really liked your speech. I learned about some accident-prevention techniques that I never knew before. You showed a lot of pep and enthusiasm through your good vocal energy, and for your next speech, you may want to concentrate on establishing more eye contact with the people who sit toward your left. Your speech was well organized, Amy. I could follow the logic of your argument." In this example, John's comments provide concrete information directly to Amy. They are also "bookended" with praise, so that Amy should feel good about her efforts as she accepts John's specific suggestions for improvement.

Conclusion

By now you are familiar with the Speech Chain. You know the difference between talking and establishing real communication, and you know the difference between listening and hearing. Finally, you are aware of the importance of feedback both during and after the speech, and you have a model of how to provide strong, positive feedback to a speaker. Now you are ready to begin preparing a speech.

2

THE GROUNDWORK

Before you can actually begin writing a speech, you need to decide what form it will take. Different types of speeches suit different occasions. For an extremely formal occasion, a speech might be memorized or read from a script. Generally, in classroom situations, students may not want to memorize an entire speech nor will they give manuscript speeches. If you memorize a speech, word for word, you run the risk of "blanking" and losing your place in the speech. If you read your speech from a manuscript, you run the risks of a stilted delivery, of being tied to a lectern or speaking stand, and of not having strong eye contact because you are looking down at a page. Therefore, an effective speech form for most situations is the extemporaneous speech. For purposes of this book, we will define *extemporaneous* as "prepared and conversational." This means that the speaker has thought through and organized the content. The speaker may have some notes, yet uses them only for reference. The speaker addresses the audience as if speaker and audience are having a conversation.

The extemporaneous speech differs from the *impromptu* speech because the extemporaneous speech requires much planning. The impromptu speech can be given "spur of the moment" with little planning. With careful preparation, knowing what you will say, and in what order you will say it, you will be able to deliver a strong, extemporaneous speech. Careful preparation, going through a process of acquiring and organizing content, and then knowing that you have something new and interesting to say are the keys to confident speech delivery.

ANALYZING YOUR AUDIENCE

When a teacher asks the students in a speech class what they think is the first step in speech preparation, they usually reply, "Choosing a topic." However, choosing a topic is actually the *second* step. Before you choose a topic, you really need to know something about your audience, the people with whom you will be communicating. You want to make sure that the topic you select will have some interest or relevance for your specific audience. Therefore, the first step in speech preparation is to analyze your audience, to consider the individuals who make up the audience and decide what their interests might be.

The first, obvious element in audience analysis is *age*. What is the age range of members of the audience? In a classroom situation, you might want to focus on topics that are especially relevant to teenagers or young adults. For example, issues that deal with current concerns such as the future of the environment or diseases, such as AIDS might be attention-getting topics for that age group.

The second element to consider is *gender*. Is the audience composed of both males and females? Some topics may be of greater interest to members of one sex or the other. For example, a talk on expanded career opportunities for young women may have little appeal to young men.

A third element to analyze is *geographical location*. What issues or concerns are particular to your part of the country? For example, a speech dealing with how to handle the effects of heavy traffic might be important to those who live in large cities, but would not be as interesting to a rural audience.

Finally, you should consider any *personal information* you can obtain regarding the specific interests or hobbies of your audience. What do they like to do in their spare time? What do they do in the summer? What are the popular activities or sports in your area? What kinds of music, radio and television programs, or films are popular? For example, if you know that many of the people in your audience enjoy dancing, an engaging topic might be a form of dancing, such as the dangers of slam dancing or moshing.

After you analyze your audience and you know to and for whom you will be speaking, you need to think about what kind of topic will engage and maintain the audience's interest, and you need to think about the specific purpose of the speech. Is it to 1.) Inform? 2.) Demonstrate a process? 3.) Persuade the audience to a point of of view? 4.) Move the audience to action? 5.) Share aspects of literature? 6.) Entertain? Typically, a first formal speech experience entails informing the audience, providing new information about a topic. Assuming that your first speech is informative, you need to select a topic that truly interests *you,* one with which you want to spend some time and about which you are curious. Informative topics may pertain to current issues or events or they can relate to a moment in history or a biography, a story about someone or a group of people. Some successful student speeches focused on topics of sexual harassment, cloning of humans, sign language, and the assassination of President John F. Kennedy.

If you have difficulty thinking of a topic that both interests you and that you think you can find information on, you may want to look in the *Reader's Guide to Periodical Literature* in your library. The *Reader's Guide* is a reference book that is organized alphabetically, by topic. It contains listings of most of the current articles published in popular periodicals. Consulting the *Reader's Guide* will provide topics that others thought were important enough about which to write.

After you choose a topic, you will need to see if you can find enough new, specific information to form the basis of an interesting speech. Gathering content takes research: locating sources and then extracting selected information from those sources to form the body of the speech. Perhaps the easiest, most typical sources to use are the various forms of printed materials. However, you may also draw on personal knowledge, interviews, and information gleaned from media sources: radio, television, and film.

GATHERING CONTENT

The first step in determining what information is available on your topic is to investigate relevant printed materials. In a library or instructional materials center (IMC), conduct a review of the literature. You may want to begin with the card catalog to see what books address your topic and if those books are available to check out of the library or IMC. From the card catalog, you can move to the *Reader's Guide to Periodical Literature* to identify titles of magazine articles recently written on the topic. Finally, you can use a computerized index, such as Infotrac or Wilson Line, if available. Some computerized indices provide more than a listing of what is available in print by title and author; they also include a summary or abstract statement. Newspapers are another source of information. They may have their own computerized index, such as Newsbank, where you can find appropriate articles.

Generally, in preparing an outline for a five-minute speech, you will want to start with a working bibliography of at least twenty sources. A working bibliography encompasses a review of the literature and is a list of potential sources. After you look up the sources to see which are actually available to you (through your library or IMC) and determine which sources contain the kind of information you believe will be useful, you may whittle the number of sources to as few as five.

How do you know which sources will be useful? How do you keep track of what information comes from which source? You may want to begin a note-taking and recording system on 3 x 5 inch or 4 x 6 inch note cards using the following method. As you construct your working bibliography—the list of all possible sources—record the sources on 3 x 5 note cards. For books, record author(s), title, copyright date, publisher, and place of publication. For periodicals, record author(s), article title, periodical title, publication date, volume number, and page numbers. For interviews, note the name and title of the interviewee and the date and location of the interview. For television and radio programs, write the name of the program, the station on which it aired, the title of the episode (if given), and the date of broadcast.

Let's take a look at the speech preparation work of Richenda, a speech class student. Richenda analyzed her audience, chose a topic, and then constructed a working bibliography on note cards to determine if she could find sufficient information to complete an outline and prepare a speech. Richenda chose the topic of the biological cloning of human beings for her informative/persuasive speech. She thought that everyone in the audience might be intrigued by the prospect of having a personal "double" created. The idea of having or being a clone is odd—and therefore interesting. Here is an example of one of Richenda's bibliography cards.

Elmer-Dewitt, Philip	A
"Cloning: Where do we draw the line?"	
<u>Time</u>	
November 8, 1993	
Volume 142	
pp. 64-67	

With the information on this bibliography card, Richenda can easily find the article by Philip Elmer-Dewitt. In the upper right-hand corner, she wrote the letter A, and will designate all of her cards with a letter of the alphabet for easy reference. After Richenda completes her bibliography cards, she will be ready to write a working thesis statement and look up the information in her sources.

FOCUSING YOUR RESEARCH

A *thesis statement* differs from a *statement of topic* because a thesis gives specific direction to the speech. The thesis is a sentence, with a subject and an attitude about that subject, that summarizes everything that the speaker will prove in the speech. For example, Richenda's topic is biological cloning of human beings. In her working thesis about cloning, the point she wants to make about her topic is that "Biological cloning of human beings has negative consequences." The subject in this thesis is, of course, "cloning" and the attitude is "negative."

For the information Richenda gleans through research to be valuable, it must relate to and support her working thesis. Choosing a working thesis before you begin to take notes can help you to focus your research. You will need to take notes on only the material that relates directly to the thesis. If you tried to take notes on everything that you found relating to the topic, you might end up with an incredible supply of information that would not support any one major point.

TAKING NOTES

You will need to take notes on the information that you find. Notes can be recorded on 4 x 6 inch cards which provide a little more space than the 3 x 5 cards have for the content of your speech.

The process of taking notes sounds easier than it is. Taking notes does not mean recording everything that you read verbatim. Good note-takers pick and choose which information they think is relevant to the thesis. They also use a variety of forms for taking notes.

Perhaps one of the best techniques for taking notes is to *paraphrase*. Paraphrasing means that you restate the author's points in your own words. One technique for paraphrasing is to read several paragraphs, then close your eyes and reflect on the significance of those paragraphs— the most important points that you can remember—and record those points. This way you avoid *plagiarism,* or taking someone else's words verbatim and using them as though they were your own.

While Richenda was taking notes for her outline and speech on cloning, she read the following passage from *Time* magazine, November 8, 1993, p. 67. This passage is referred to on her bibliography card.

Arthur Caplan, director of the Center for Bioethics at the University of Minnesota, could conjure up several equally defensible ways in which cloning embryos might be medically appropriate. Suppose, for example, a woman knew she was about to become sterile, either because of chemotherapy or through exposure to toxic substances. She might consider having an embryo cloned for future use. Or suppose a couple knew that their children had a chance of inheriting hemophilia or cystic fibrosis. Researchers have developed DNA-analysis techniques to screen embryos for such disorders, but the procedures require snipping cells off embryos, a process that sometimes kills them. In such situations, having a couple of extra clones around could mean the difference between passing on a defective gene or giving birth to a perfectly health child.

On her 4 x 6 notecard from this source,
Richenda paraphrased what she had read.
The note card reads as follows:

A p. 67 + uses
Arthur Caplan, Center for Bioethics, University of Minn.,
    If a woman knew she'd be sterile because of chemical
or toxic exposure, she might want an embryo.
    If a couple knows their kids will have hemophilia or
cystic fibrosis, DNA researchers can cut cells off the embryos.
Cutting cells off can kill them. Cloning can make the difference
between transmitting a defective gene and having a
healthy baby.   [paraphrase]

Richenda's note card heading is a form of
shorthand. The letter A refers to the bibliography
card that contains all the source information for
the *Time* magazine article. The page number indicates where she found the specific information.
The title "+ uses" summarizes the focus of the information on the card, "positive uses of cloning."
On the bottom of the card, Richenda wrote the

word "paraphrase" to remind her that she had read a paragraph and then put that paragraph into her own words on the card.

Good notes may take many forms. For example, summarizing important aspects of an article is a good way to record information. A summary is usually a brief statement of main points. Additionally, by writing down direct quotations or statistics, you can store concrete information to support a point of view. On the next note card example, from the *Time* magazine article on cloning, November 8, 1993, Richenda combined a summary with direct quotations and statistics.

A, pp. 65, 66   opinions

"Do you think human cloning is a good thing?"
Yes - 14% No - 75%
"Would you have liked to have been a clone?"
Yes - 6% No 86%

Telephone poll of 500 adults by Time/CNN, October 28, 1993, by Yankelovich Partners, Inc.

"Cloning: Where Do We Draw the Line?" by Philip Elmer DeWitt in TIME, November 8, 1993. Copyright © 1993 by TIME Inc. Reprinted by Permission.

In the two note card examples shown here, Richenda used a variety of forms to record information. She paraphrased, she summarized, and she directly recorded quotations and statistics. She did not copy what she read in source materials word for word, except for quotations and statistics. Because she carefully selected which material she recorded, she completed an important step in gathering information useful to her purpose and in making that information her own. By keying her note cards to her bibliography cards, Richenda ensures that when she writes her outline and needs to document sources in her endnotes and in her bibliography, all of the information will be easily available. She also documented which material she took from which sources so that she can provide proper citations later. In this way, she avoids committing plagiarism.

As you gather content for a speech, you will need to use a system that helps you to organize major points as you record information. Using 3 x 5 note cards for source information and 4 x 6 note cards for specific content keyed to source cards may help you to stay focused and organized. This system can also be used for sources other than written text, such as radio interviews, personal interviews, and television programs. The key is to think through which content will be most important in supporting your working thesis. Then use a technique, such as paraphrasing or summarizing, to record content. Finally, be aware of which technique you used. If you jot down which type of technique you used, you will become attuned to your own working style, and you will remember how the content you recorded relates to the original text itself.

For a typical five- to ten-minute speech, you will need approximately five to ten research sources from which to obtain viable, usable information. You will also need approximately fifty note cards from which to pick and choose information to support a thesis. You may need more sources and more specific content, or you may need fewer to fill out your speech. If you overprepare in terms of obtaining content, you can easily edit. Stretching content to fill an allotted time limit is much more difficult. Make sure that you take the time to search for new, interesting information and that you organize that information so that listeners can follow your thoughts.

Conclusion

Now that you know the first steps in speech preparation—how to analyze the audience, choose a topic, and gather information—you need to think about how you will organize the content of your speech.

3

THE BODY OF
YOUR SPEECH

A speech, similar to a written theme, has three major divisions: introduction, body, and conclusion. The body contains the bulk of your message, the meat or substance of the speech. One efficient way to prepare your speech content is to outline the speech body, and then write your introduction and conclusion separately, in paragraph form.

THE BODY OF YOUR SPEECH 29

ORGANIZING YOUR CONTENT

When you give a speech, the listeners get only one chance to hear it. They need to be able to follow the pattern of your thinking. To present your content in a way that is easy for your listeners to follow, you must organize it carefully. The process of determining your organizational scheme, clustering your content, and writing your outline will enable you to clarify your own thinking before you present your message to others. With solid preparation in gathering and organizing content, you will gain both familiarity and confidence about what you are going to say so that, during the speech, you can concentrate on how you are presenting the content—on your delivery. Your outline can serve as a guide to the order in which you will present content as you prepare your final speaking notes.

Once you gather enough specific information on your topic, you can begin to organize it according to a pattern so that your listeners can make sense of what you have to say. Some typical methods of organization include the following:

Spatial: classifying by location in space, such as east to west, highest to lowest, farthest to nearest, and so on.

Comparison-Contrast: showing the similarities and differences between various facets of your subject.

Climactic: building from the the least important or exciting point to the most exciting or important point.

Order of Importance: moving from the most important to the least important point.

Topical: dividing the thesis into aspects of the topic—subdivisions of the subject matter arbitrarily chosen—to form content headings.

Chronological: (Chronos was the Greek god of time), presenting content in order of time, from beginning to middle to end of an event or events.

Cause-effect-solution or problem-solution: describing a problem and convincing listeners either that the problem exists or that a course of action will lead to a solution of the problem. This type of organization is often used for persuasive speeches.

The type of organization you choose depends on the purpose or type of the speech and the specific content you have gathered.

For example, among your first speeches may be one based on personal experience. For this type of speech, instead of doing library research to obtain content, you must look into yourself for something engaging and relevant to share with your audience. After analyzing what your audience's interests might be, you can choose a topic about one of your experiences to arouse their attention and curiosity. This type of speech often lends itself to *chronological* organization.

In order to decide which type of organization your content most logically fits into, you should examine your note cards and sort them according to their topic headings. As Richenda was taking notes, she headed her note cards with a few words to summarize the content on each. Those words are the *note card topic headings.*

CLUSTERING YOUR CONTENT

Some students like to take the information on their note cards and cluster it to see if it falls into logical categories, one leading to another. If

Richenda had clustered her information on
cloning, the clusters might have looked like this:

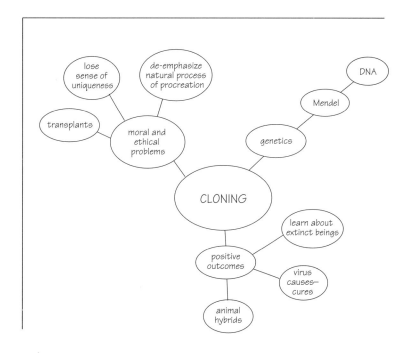

Looking at the clusters of Richenda's content,
you can see the three major categories into
which the content falls. Therefore, Richenda
chose to create an outline divided by topics,
thereby giving her content a *topical* organization.
Richenda's three topics make up the major
divisions of her thesis statement. As a result,

Richenda's thesis statement becomes, "Although biological cloning can have positive effects in medicine and agriculture, cloning of human beings is difficult to do and would have negative consequences." Judging by her clusters and the way her speech content naturally falls into three categories, her topic sentences will address the history or past practices of cloning, the few positive outcomes of cloning experiments, and the moral problems (negative consequences) that cloning could cause.

DEVELOPING AN OUTLINE

When thinking about how to outline and about which sentence goes where in the outline, imagine a device called the "Ladder of Abstraction." The Ladder of Abstraction is narrow at the bottom and broad at the top to illustrate how in good speaking, as in good writing, you must move from general to specific information to communicate effectively.

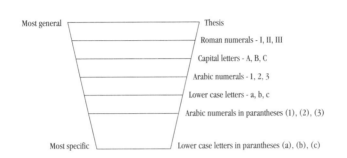

Most general — Thesis
Roman numerals - I, II, III
Capital letters - A, B, C
Arabic numerals - 1, 2, 3
Lower case letters - a, b, c
Arabic numerals in parantheses (1), (2), (3)
Most specific — Lower case letters in parantheses (a), (b), (c)

As you outline the body of your speech, every sentence that you write must in some way support your thesis. After you write the thesis, which is the most general statement you will make in your outline and which appears at the top of the Ladder of Abstraction, the next sentences you write will be called *topic sentences*. They indicate the major divisions of your content. Depending upon how long and detailed your outline is, you may then move to the next most concrete level, the *subtopic sentences,* or you may move directly to the detail level. Details are the most specific, concrete elements in the content of your speech. They are the examples, illustrations, personal experiences, statistics, quotations, and analogies that will form the substance of your speech and make it new and interesting.

In setting up your outline, use Roman numerals to signify the most general or abstract concepts, and capital letters to denote the next most general statements. Moving down the ladder, Arabic numerals signify the next more concrete concepts, and lower case letters designate the most concrete or specific concepts. In longer works, outlining can continue with Arabic numerals and lower case letters in parentheses and brackets, but our examples will not be long enough to require these notations. The Ladder of Abstraction illustrates how the most general statements (except for the thesis) are signified with Roman numerals and how the most specific statements receive number and letter designations.

The following is an edited version of how Richenda organized her content into an outline so that all of her specific information relates to her thesis statement. Notice in the outline how she moves from general points to specific information from her research to support those points. You may also notice that the endnotes in the outline start with the number 3. That is because the first two endnotes were for material found in the introductory paragraph to Richenda's speech. The introduction to this speech, complete with endnote numbers, appears on page 70.

Thesis: Although biological cloning can have positive effects in medicine and agriculture, cloning of human beings is difficult to do and would have negative consequences.

I. The difficult task of cloning, or making an identical twin of an organism, has been a subject of scientific study for many years.

   A. The modern understanding of genetics did not develop until 1866, when an Augustinian monk published a book on how human traits are transmitted.[3]

      1. The monk, Gregor Mendel, discovered genes and studied chromosomes, the storage cells of human characteristics.

      2. This early look at deoxyribonucleic acid, or DNA, which stores an organism's genetic information inside the chromosomes, allowed scientists to learn that the double structure lets the chromosomes split and copy during cell division.[4]

B. Much later, scientists struggled with cloning different life-forms.

   1. Steen Willadsen first split an embryo and implanted each half in a sheep, which resulted in a successful cloning.

   2. In 1972, a live offspring was developed from a frozen, cloned mouse embryo.[5]

C. In 1993, Robert J. Stillman and Jerry Hall announced the division of seventeen human embryos into forty-eight clones.

   1. The cells stopped dividing after six days because of an abnormal embryo.[6]

   2. This experiment led to international controversy about the ethics of creating human life in this way.

      a. The procedure was banned in Britain, Japan, and Germany.

      b. A spokesperson for the Japanese Medical Association said the experiment was "unthinkable."

      c. French President Francois Mitterand
        was "horrified."

      d. The Vatican's *L'Osservatore Romano* ran
        an editorial that said that further
        experimentation would
        lead into a "tunnel
        of madness."[7]

II. In their research, biologists have
found some positive uses for cloning.

  A. Animal embryos have been cloned for hybrid
    purposes.

    1. Cloning embryos could reduce livestock
      costs and fewer embryos would be
      needed.[8]

    2. Canadian researchers have cloned calf
      embryos to increase by eight times the
      number of offspring a milk cow can
      bear.[9]

  B. Some scientists use DNA cloning to search
    for the causes and cures
    of viruses.[10]

1. The viruses that caused the 1918
   influenza epidemic are being cloned to
   prevent other outbreaks.[11]
2. Genetic cloning could also be used to
   discover embryonic warning signs of
   other diseases, such
   as AIDS.[12]

C. Through cloning, scientists may learn about
   extinct beings.

   1. As in *Jurassic Park*, paleontologists are
      investigating and sequencing the DNA in
      120 million-year-old beetles stuck
      in amber.[13]
   2. DNA was also cloned from a 40,000-year-
      old woolly mammoth, 5,000-year-old
      Egyptian mummies, a 7,500
      year-old Floridian Indian, and
      a magnolia leaf over 17 million years
      old.[14]

D. Cloning may help infertile people to
   have children.

        1. Couples wishing for a surrogate child or fetal implant could choose a clone of a child already grown to see how the child may adjust to their family.

        2. The clone may then be placed inside of the womb.

III. Cloning human embryos would cause significant moral and ethical problems.

  A. If successfully cloned, life-forms might be patented as material objects and put on the market.[15]

      1. This worries Professor Ruth Macklin who states, "If there was a market in it—people do all kinds of things for money."[16]

      2. Another concern is that a black market may develop for cloned embryos.

  B. Cloned embryos could be used for transplants; however, the person might have to grow up first.

1. If a clone is needed for the transplant of a heart or eye, a mother could give birth to the clone and care for it until it is of age to donate the body part.[17]
2. Otherwise, doctors might interfere with the clone when it has been in the mother's uterus for six weeks to remove the higher brain cells so the baby would lose the capacity to think.[18]

C. Individuals may lose their sense of uniqueness with numerous twins in the world or in their own family.

1. In one study, 350 pairs of identical twins retained most of the same personality traits no matter how they were reared.[19]
2. Producing many copies of one person would decrease our sense of wonder at individuality and diversity.[20]

D. Reproducing clones of children in petri dishes would de-emphasize the natural process of procreation and family planning.

    1. An imbalance of males and females might be created because of too much cloning of one gender.

    2. A "bad chromosome" could sneak by to give many children in the family the same disease.[21]

E. No one knows who should should be responsible for deciding which embryos should be cloned and reproduced.

    1. Jeremy Rifkin, a biotechnology critic, showed his concern by asking, "At what point do we move from trying to cure horrible genetic disease to trying to enhance genetic traits?"[22]

    2. Physiologist Marie DiBerardino agreed that she's "morally against manipulating genetic material that would develop into a whole human being." She stated, "We just don't have the right to manipulate the gene pool of human individuals."[23]

Although Richenda's outline may appear to be lengthy and detailed, the content and organization in the outline will help her to give a truly organized, substantive speech.

When Rachel was assigned to give a five-minute personal experience speech, she decided to talk about her experience working in a soup kitchen for the homeless. Rachel's thesis involved her self-discovery through the experience: "After working in a soup kitchen, I discovered that I had been living a sheltered life of luxuries." Rachel's outline of the body of her speech follows. Notice how well chronological organization works for this type of speech.

I. When my mother first said that we were going to help out in a city soup kitchen for homeless people, I wasn't exactly happy about the idea.

    A. I had never before been around people who were really poor.

        1. I was frightened because I had no idea what to expect when I got to the soup kitchen.

2. I was afraid of the poor people who would be coming to the soup kitchen because I had no idea of how to act around them.

B. I did not want to spend my time feeding strangers food when all my friends were having sleep-over parties and going ice skating.

1. When my mom first told me that we were going to help, I started to cry because I couldn't understand why all my friends got to go out and have a great time while I had to spend my time with homeless people.

2. I was also angry that I had to give up my free time for people who I thought could not find jobs and would not take baths.

C. I was also afraid of going into a neighborhood of poverty.

1. I had always heard that places where poor people lived were filled with drug dealers.

        2. I had also heard that many of these
           people could be violent.

II. When we arrived at the soup kitchen I was still
    a little frightened but was reassured when I
met the other volunteers.

    A. The other helpers were really friendly.

        1. I started talking to my co-workers and
           found that I was having a great time.

        2. I was soon preparing food and laughing
           with the rest of the volunteers at my
           mother's jokes.

    B. I had great conversations with others who
       were about my age.

        1. Brad, Lindy, and I talked about how
           our parents had made us "volunteer"
           and how we hadn't wanted to come.

        2. We talked about how we were afraid of
           the people and didn't know what to
           expect.

III. When the homeless people started to arrive I
    felt relaxed and good about what I was doing.

    A. As the people lined up for food, I
       noticed the great number and variety of
       individuals who were homeless.

      1. At least five hundred people arrived
         for food.

      2. The people had many different
         nationalities and ages.

      3. Many of the children had ripped
         clothing and looked as if they were
         starving.

   B. While I worked at my station handing out
      milk, I was surprised at the attitudes of
      many of the people.

      1. When I tried to talk to some of the
         people they wouldn't respond to me;
         they just lowered their heads and
         kept walking.

      2. I felt as if I had said or done
         something wrong.

      3. My mother explained that these people
         were ashamed that they had to take
         handouts.

IV. After everyone had been fed I started to think
  about what had taken place.

   A. I thought about how I had helped other
      people.

      1. I was proud of what I had done.

        2. I was also depressed after witnessing the situations of so many unfortunate people.

   B. After we returned home the experience was still on my mind.

        1. I felt depressed that night because I couldn't stop thinking about the faces of the people I had served.

        2. I also felt guilty because I knew that I would sleep in a warm, comfortable house and many of the people I had served might be sleeping outside on a park bench or in the street.

V. That day and in the following weeks, I learned about my own values.

   A. I realized that life is about more than cars and money.

        1. I had always thought that what you had made up what you were.

        2. I see things differently after seeing people who have so little yet are willing to wait in line to feed their children.

```
B. I started changing some of my views.
   1. I felt that life was about much more
      than my little suburban world.
   2. I also decided that I wanted to work
      toward changing systems in our
      society to prevent people from
      ending up homeless.
```

Rachel divided her chronological outline into sections about her feelings before working in the soup kitchen, during the experience, and after the experience. In addition to describing the experience of feeding the homeless people, Rachel explains how the activity affected her feelings and values. Just as Richenda's topical outline on cloning divided her content into logical categories, Rachel's chronological outline helped her to give a well-organized, easy-to-follow speech.

USING VERBAL
SUPPORTING MATERIAL

During their speeches, both Richenda and Rachel elaborated on the written material in their outlines. While speaking, they went into greater depth and detail about specific content than their outlines contained. They used a variety of verbal supporting material to clarify major points. *Verbal supporting material* should comprise much of the body of the speech. The types of verbal support that most speakers will use can be broken into some general categories. Whichever categories or types you use, you must make sure that the content is vivid, specific and concrete.

One of the most typical forms of verbal support in a speech is the explanation. You will give a statement and then explain how or why it is true. Explanations often answer the following questions: Who? What? Where? When? Why? How? Here is an example of how explanation can clarify a point from Steve's speech about the Chicago Cubs. Steve's thesis is: "Everyone should root for the Chicago Cubs." One of his topic sentences in the outline and major points in the speech revolved around the exciting media broadcasts of Cubs games.

Explanation:

WGN is the home of many exciting, hilarious announcers. The late Bert Wilson, an optimistic middle-aged man, was the first broadcaster to become excited when the Cubs were winning. Lou Boudreau often humored his audience by mispronouncing names. The emotional Vince Lloyd occasionally lost his voice while announcing thrilling moments. One of the best-known Cub broadcasters was the eternally optimistic Jack "Hey Hey" Brickhouse who announced for the Cubs from 1948 until 1980. Perhaps the most flamboyant, funniest Cubs announcer is the unofficial "Mayor of Rush Street" Harry "Holy Cow" Caray who leaves the fans in stitches when he sings "Take Me Out to the Ball Game" during the seventh inning stretch.

Steve's explanation answered the questions who made the broadcasts exciting? and why were they exciting? Even if you are unfamiliar with the specific broadcasters, concrete information about announcers who mispronounce names or sing during part of the game can help to explain the point about exciting broadcasts.

Another type of verbal support is *illustration,* or telling a story to emphasize a point. The illustrations can be hypothetical (made up) or factual. Consider how illustrations might work to support Rachel's topic, her experience feeding homeless people.

Hypothetical Illustration:

> Imagine that you you are homeless and hungry, and that you have no money to buy food. You hear that a soup kitchen will provide meals to poor, indigent people. You journey to the kitchen, and after standing in line behind hundreds of other people who need assistance, it is your turn to receive a meal. As a volunteer hands you a carton of milk, you look up to say thank you, but your eyes and the volunteer's do not meet. You lower your head in embarrassment and shame for finding yourself in these circumstances.

This illustration places listeners in a hypothetical situation and asks them to relate to the feelings involved in the situation. The more vivid and specific the illustration is, the more easily listeners will be able to identify with the story.

Factual Illustration (first person):

    The first day I worked at the soup kitchen, the sky was overcast and gloomy, to match my mood. As the doors opened and the homeless people filed in to receive food, I couldn't believe how many of them were standing in line. Although I lost count, at least 500 ragged, tired-looking individuals were waiting for some help. As I handed milk cartons to two teenaged girls, I tried to look into their faces to see what they were feeling. They wouldn't look at me; they passed through my station with downcast eyes. When I asked my mother about their lack of expression, she explained that the girls might have been embarrassed because they had to ask for food.

This illustration is a real story; it is based in fact. In this case, the story was told in the first person, however, although factual illustrations can be based on personal experiences, they do not have to be. The same story could be told in the third person, if it had been obtained through an interview or other research.

Factual illustration (third person):

The first day that Rachel worked at the soup
kitchen the sky was overcast and gloomy, to match
her mood. As the doors opened and the homeless
people filed in to receive food, Rachel couldn't
believe how many were standing in line. Although
she lost count, at least 500 ragged, tired-looking
individuals were waiting for some help. As she
handed milk cartons to two teenaged girls, she
tried to look into their faces to see what they
were feeling. The girls wouldn't look at Rachel;
they passed through her station with downcast eyes.
When Rachel asked her mother about the girls' lack
of expression, her mother explained that they might
have been embarrassed because they had to ask food.

Once again, in telling a story to support a
general point, the more specific your detail,
the more meaningful the story will be. Because
people can relate to stories about other people,
illustrations can add "human interest" to
the speech.

Specific *examples* also support general points
well. In using examples, you move down the
Ladder of Abstraction to the concrete level and

you can impart to listeners the significance of the general points. Th following is a model from Steve's speech on the Chicago Cubs.

```
Example:
      Throughout the years, many unusual events have
occurred at Chicago Cubs games. For example, in
June of 1895, a religious group held up play in the
third inning of a Cubs game. The entire Cubs team
was arrested for contributing to the formation of a
large crowd on Sunday. Then in 1907, several
policemen had to shoot bullets into the air to
prevent a New York mob from hanging the Cubs from
lampposts after the Cubs beat the New York Giants.
The next year, the entire Cubs infield chased an
umpire off the field for making a bad call.
```

In the preceding sample, the statement about "many unusual events" is fairly general. By citing a number of specific examples of the events, the speaker provides concrete images to which the listeners can relate. Good speeches are often peppered with examples to give life to their messages.

The use of concrete *evidence* to back up generalizations can give weight to your statements. Because statistics, surveys, studies, and reports suggest research and factual proof, they are valid forms of verbal support. Any time that you use statistics, surveys, or study reports, you must give credit to your sources to make the use of specific evidence credible and believable. (For more about giving proper credit, see pages 59–61.)

Evidence:

    According to a recent study conducted by the American Cancer Society, one out of every six people will develop skin cancer in his or her lifetime. The greatest concern is malignant melanoma, the most dangerous kind of skin cancer. Incidence of melanoma among the general population doubled in the 1980s. The Environmental Protection Agency reported that for every 1 percent loss of the ozone layer, another 200,000 cases of skin cancer develop which increases skin cancer deaths by 3 to 6 percent. A 5 percent decrease of the ozone layer will increase the incidence of skin cancer as much as 20 percent in the next twenty years.

The preceding paragraph provides evidence to support the thesis that people should avoid exposure to the sun. In an outline, the statistics and survey results would require source citations (footnotes, endnotes, or other forms). To give credit during the speech, you would simply have to introduce your source(s) with a phrase such as *according to.* Anyone can present a value judgment or generalization; providing specific evidence to support that judgment gives your statements weight and believability.

Another way to add authority to your speech is to use *quotations* or *testimony* for verbal support. The words of other people, especially if they are well known or experts in a field, can help to make your position more believable.

Testimony:

Chicago Cubs fans help to make the experience of attending Cubs games truly enjoyable. Many Cubs fans are lovable diehards who attend every game of the year and root for the Cubs, day in and day out. According to Ferguson Jenkins, former Chicago Cubs pitcher, "The fans who sit in the Wrigley Field bleachers are the most ecstatic of all baseball fans."

Although some listeners may believe the statement about how wonderful the Cubs fans are, what really clinches it is Ferguson Jenkin's quotation. After all, he pitched for the Cubs, and he traveled around the league, playing games in a variety of ballparks. His quotation, his testimony, helps to make the point real and valid.

Another form of support is to explain something by comparing it with something else. Such an *analogy,* or comparison demonstrating similarities, often between something known or familiar and something less well known, can help to illustrate a point.

Analogy or Comparison:

Tanning of the skin, which some people think is an indication of good health, is actually a sign of damage done to the skin caused by ultraviolet radiation. Sometimes tanning can lead to premature aging of the skin. The effects of the sun can cause wrinkling and withering. Just as a grape becomes a raisin, too much sun can make a face look like a prune.

Analogies can make writing and speaking easier to follow and more colorful. They can also help to create images. Talking about wrinkles describes the effect of too much sun; comparing a face to a prune creates a vivid mental picture to illustrate the same point. The more you use language to illustrate what you mean, as opposed to merely describing what you mean, the more vivid and alive your speech will be.

CITING SOURCES

Much of the content in your outline and in your verbal supporting material comes from research sources. In the outline itself, you must give credit to those sources to acknowledge the work of others and to help you remember from where your content came from.

Direct quotations (someone else's words copied verbatim), and statistics (numbers used to prove a point) must receive citations. Original thoughts must also be credited, but are more difficult to distinguish. Therefore, you must use your judgment to determine whether an idea is unusual enough to cite its source. If you think that an idea might be general knowledge, a citation is unnecessary. However, if you think that an idea originated with one of your sources, you will need to acknowledge the writer(s) of that source. By giving credit to the source, the writer avoids *plagiarism,* the taking of another's ideas and passing them off as one's own.

In her outline on the topic of cloning, Richenda used endnotes to acknowledge her sources. After each direct quotation, statistic, or unusual new idea that she culled from her sources, Richenda placed a number corresponding to a complete source listing on a separate page at the end of the outline called the endnote page. She also compiled a complete bibliography, or list of all the sources she used to acquire information. To give proper credit to sources, you need to have a system to keep track of which information comes from which original work. Keying bibliography cards to note cards, as Richenda did, through an alphabetical or some other system, is therefore important.

Richenda's endnotes and bibliography for her outline on her speech on human cloning follow here. The endnotes correlate citations in her text to show where she obtained concrete pieces of information. The bibliography is a general listing of all the sources she used.

ENDNOTES

1. Shannon Brownlee, "Send in the Clones," <u>U.S. News and World Report</u>, November 8, 1993, 24.

2. Philip Elmer-Dewitt, "Cloning, Where Do We Draw the Line?,' <u>Time</u>, November 8, 1993, 68.

3. Joel Swerdlow, "The Double-edged Helix," <u>Wilson Quarterly</u>, Spring 1992, 63.

4. Swerdlow, 63.

5. Elmer-Dewitt, 67.

6. Elmer-Dewitt, 66.

7. Elmer-Dewitt, 65.

8. Marie-Christine Comte, "(Live)Stock Options," <u>Ceres</u>, November/December 1992, 16.

9. Geoffrey Cowley, "Clone Hype." <u>Newsweek</u>, November 8, 1993, 61.

10. Jerold M. Lowenstein, "The Remaking of the President," <u>Discover</u>, August 1991, 18.

11. Philip E. Ross, "Jurassic Virus?", <u>Scientific American</u>, October 1993, 28.

12. Ross, 28.

13. Ross, 28.

14. Begley, 56.

15. Barbara Ehrenreich, "The Economics of Cloning," <u>Time</u>, November 22, 1993, 86.

16. David Gelman, "How Will the Clone Feel?," <u>Newsweek</u>, November 8, 1993, 66.

17. Bill Lauren, "Bionic Body Building, The Ultimate Life Insurance, A Clone," <u>Longevity</u>, January 1991, 24.

18. Lauren, 25.

19. "Heredity, They'll be the Same but Different," <u>Newsweek</u>, November 8, 1993 , 62.

20. Richard A. McCormick, "Should We Clone Humans? Wholeness, Individuality, Reverence, " <u>The Christian Century</u>, November 1993, 1148.

21. McCormick, 1148.

22. Lauren, 26.

23. Swerdlow, 67.

All of the sources listed in Richenda's end-notes are magazine periodicals. Periodicals are good sources of concrete information for a short speech. A bibliography lists all of the sources from which you gathered information in alphabetical order, not just the ones from which you took quotations, statistics, or other concrete support. .

BIBLIOGRAPHY

Adler, Jerry. "Clone Hype." <u>Newsweek</u>, November 8, 1993, volume 122, 60-63.

Begley, Sharon. "Here Come the DNAsaurs." <u>Newsweek</u>, June 14, 1993, volume 121, 56.

Brownlee, Shannon. "Send in the Clones." <u>U.S. News and World Report</u>, November 8, 1993, volume 115, 24-25.

"Cloning Around." <u>The Economist</u>. October 30, 1993, volume 328, 948.

Comti, Marie-Christine. "(Live)Stock Options." <u>Ceres</u>, November/December 1991, 15-19.

Cowley, Geoffrey, with Mary Hager and Joshua
   Cooper Ramo. "The View from the Womb:
   Babies to Order Remain a Pipe Dream." <u>Newsweek</u>,
   November 8, 1993, volume 142, 86.

Ehrenreich, Barbara. "The Economics of Cloning."
   <u>Time</u>, November 22, 1993, volume 142, 86.

Elmer-Dewitt, Philip. "Cloning: Where Do We Draw
   the Line?" <u>Time</u>, November 8, 1993,
   volume 142, 64-67.

Fackelman, Kathy A. "Researchers 'clone'
   Human Embryos." <u>Science News</u>, October 30,
   1993, 276.

Gelman, David. "How Will the Clone Feel?" <u>Newsweek</u>,
   November 8 1993, volume 122, 65-66.

Home Medical Encyclopedia. 1989. s.v. "DNA."
   "Jekyll and Jekyll." <u>The Economist</u>, October 30,
   1993, 20-21.

Lauren, Bill. "Bionic Body Building: The Ultimate
   Life Insurance: A Clone." <u>Longevity</u>, January
   1991, 22-27.

Lowenstein, Jerold M. "The Remaking of the
   President." <u>Discover</u>, August 1991, 18-22.

McCormick, Richard A. "Should We Clone Humans?
Wholeness, Individuality, Reverence." The
Christian Century, November 17, 1993,
volume 110, 1148-1150.

Merz, Beverly. "The Genetics Revolution: Designer
Genes." American Health, March 1993, 46-54.

Ross, Philip E. "Jurassic Virus" Scientific
American, October 1993, volume 269, 28.

"Science." Time, November 8, 1993, volume 142, 27.

Swerdlow, Joel L. "The Double-edged Helix." Wilson
Quarterly, Spring 1992, 60-67.

A bibliography may take one of several forms that are currently acceptable. In some cases punctuation varies, and in some cases you may use a different heading for both the endnote and bibliography pages. The most important point is that the last step of preparing the outline of the speech body is to cite the works used according to a definite and consistent form.

Now that you have gathered information and organized and documented the body of your speech, you need to start thinking about how to begin and end it. You are now ready to plan your introduction and conclusion.

4

CHAPTER

THE INTRODUCTION AND CONCLUSION

What is the single most important part of your speech? It is the walk to the front of the group and the opening lines of the speech. During those opening sentences, you will determine whether the audience will listen to your speech or tune out you and your message. A good introduction is crucial to the success of your speech.

No matter where you give your speech, even if you are in a classroom where you have a captive audience, no one really *has* to listen to you. Your job, as a speaker, is to make the audience *want* to listen, to grab and hold their attention throughout the speech. You must use your introduction to engage your audience's attention.

The introduction presents not only your topic, but you as well. Therefore you must establish a favorable first impression so that audience members want to listen, not merely hear, your speech. The introduction also provides a preview of what you will cover in the speech body, indicates the specific purpose of the speech, and relates the topic to the audience. The end of the introduction should provide a transition into the speech body. In other words, the introduction sets the tone for the rest of the speech.

PREPARING AN ATTENTION-GETTING INTRODUCTION

Good introductions take many forms. Generally, the minimum length is three sentences, but, depending on how much explanation you want to give, the introduction can be as long as ten or fifteen sentences. There are many ways to spark an audience's attention and begin a speech effectively. The suggestions that follow are among the most frequently used and successful methods for introducing a speech.

To attract the audience's attention immediately, relate the topic directly to them in the opening line. Or, appeal to audience self-interest as an effective starter. Try using visual aids or properties to engage your audience. If you give audience members something to look at (in addition to you), you may enhance their visual focus.

Consider the introduction Richenda wrote for her speech on cloning entitled "Biological Cloning: A Two-Way Mirror."

[Richenda holds up a mirror, looks at herself and then holds up the mirror to the audience.]

"Does looking at yourself violate some profound sense of self and individuality?" Mary Martin, Director of the Fertility Program at the University of California told a *U.S. News and World Report* interviewer that she has been pondering this notion for awhile.[1] Yet, she is not speaking about the reflection of yourself in the mirror, but about a real-live human being made as a copy of you through biological cloning. Cloning, creating an exact duplicate of a living thing, has been accomplished with various plants and animals. However, the possibility of biological cloning of human beings has created a great deal of controversy. In a recent *Time* magazine telephone survey, 58 percent of the 500 people surveyed questioned the morality of cloning.[2] Although biological cloning can have positive effects in medicine and agriculture, cloning of human beings is difficult to do and would have negative consequences.

In her introduction, Richenda asks a pertinent question to arouse curiosity. She also uses a visual aid, the mirror, to capture attention.

Finally, the last line of the introduction, the thesis statement, provides a clear preview of the major point Richenda will focus on in the speech. Richenda's opening words truly fulfill the purposes of a good introduction.

Suspense works well in an introduction to capture the audience's attention. If you tease your audience a bit by making them guess what you are talking about, you may arouse their curiosity and entice them to want to listen. You can build suspense with a sequence of opening statements or questions that build to your thesis while encouraging audience members to speculate on or mentally predict your next statement.

As musician and comedian Victor Borge says, "The shortest distance between two people is laughter." A humorous introduction will definitely establish a desire to listen. If you can stimulate laughter, you will create an atmosphere in which the audience is with you as you speak. One word of caution: Trying to be funny is risky. If you attempt to tell a joke or humorous anecdote, the humor may fall flat. Audience reaction may range from a few sparse chuckles to groans to silence.

(Silence is probably the worst reaction of all to a would-be joke.) If you attempt humor, you'll need to be happy with *any* reaction. If the joke falls flat, go right on with the body of the speech.

Here is the introduction from Steve's speech about the Chicago Cubs. Notice how he uses a series of questions to create suspense. After the third question, audience members should be wondering, "What team is he talking about?" The comments about the record of the Cubs then add a touch of wry humor. The introduction ends with a statement of thesis.

What team in sports history has won more games than any other? And what team has been in existence the longest? And what team has by far the most dedicated following in baseball? You guessed it, sports fans, the Chicago Cubs: America's team. Why, you might ask, do I put myself through unnecessary torture by rooting for a loser like the Cubs? I don't know; maybe it's a disease. But whatever it is, being a Cubs fan is fun. It is excitement. The Cubs have provided throngs of people, old and young, with thrilling and heartbreaking moments. So what if they never win? So what if they're in the middle of an eighty-five-year dry spell? Who cares if they haven't won a World Series since the invention of the automobile? They're still great fun; there's never a dull moment with the Cubs. Everyone should root for the Chicago Cubs.

Posing a challenge might provide a strong incentive for the audience to listen to your message. In your introduction you can dare your audience to disagree with you by the end of the speech, or you can challenge them that they will take a certain point of view or be able to do something that they could not do if they did not listen to the speech. In the following introduction from a demonstration speech on juggling, the challenge is explicit: "Listen and you can do it."

In a book entitled *Juggling for the Complete Klutz*, juggling is described as "a form of insanity everyone has the right to experience." The insanity comes in

different stages, from learning to get three balls to
jump in circles in your hands to getting sticks to
jump around in different patterns. But with the
"insanity" comes fun and challenge. Juggling is a fun
and beneficial hobby, after you master the basics.
I challenge each of you to master the basics of
juggling. I believe that each of you can learn to
juggle, and I can prove it.

The challenge or dare in the preceding introduction comes in the last two sentences. If the
speaker says "I can prove it," audience members
may respond mentally by thinking, "Oh, no you
can't." At any rate, if the introduction engages
members of the audience in a mental dialogue
or controversy with the speaker, it will pull
them into the content of the speech.

Story or illustration can be an effective beginning for a speech. As with verbal supporting material, the story can be hypothetical or factual. Its
point of view can also vary: you can tell a story
in the first person, the second person, or the
third person. The following introduction is from

a speech entitled "The Dark Side of the Sun." Notice how Peter uses a hypothetical illustration from a second person point of view to interest the audience in the content of his speech.

Imagine yourself getting ready for a nice day at the beach. You have your towel and your bathing suit ready to go, and you're waiting for your friends. When they arrive you shout "Good-bye" to your mom, and you sprint out the door. On your way out, you hear your mom ask if you have taken sunscreen with you. You yell back "yeah," knowing very well that you didn't even think about bringing any. You get to the beach; the sun is bright and hot. You and your friends enjoy a wonderful day, but the next day you notice that your shoulders really hurt. A bad sunburn, you conclude. "It will go away," you say to yourself. Eventually, the pain does go away, but you notice a small mole forming on your shoulder. It grows larger and larger, and begins to ooze. When you visit a dermatologist and he does a biopsy, it turns out to be a malignant melanoma, the most dangerous kind of skin cancer. It is removed surgically, but your whole life has been changed because you didn't protect yourself against the harmful effects of the sun. Unfortunately, your initial lack of concern about the sun's effects is a typical attitude shared by many. People should take more action to prevent health problems as a result of overexposure to the sun.

This hypothetical story, leading up to the climax of discovering cancer, speaks directly to audience members. Any one of them could be in the same situation. Here is the same introductory story told from the third person point of view.

Peter remembers the last day he spent at the beach. As his friends arrived to pick him up, he shouted "Good-bye" to his mom. On his way out, he heard his mom ask if he had taken sunscreen with him. He yelled back "yeah," knowing very well that he didn't even think about taking any. At the beach, the sun was nice and hot. Although Peter and his friends enjoyed a wonderful day, the next day he noticed that his shoulders really hurt. A bad sunburn, he concluded. "It will go away," he said to himself. Eventually, the pain did go away, but he noticed a small mole forming on his shoulder. It grew larger and larger and began to ooze. When he visited a dermatologist, and the sore was biopsied, it turned out to be a malignant melanoma, the most dangerous kind of skin cancer. The melanoma was removed surgically, but Peter's whole life had changed because he hadn't protected himself from the hazardous effects of the sun. Unfortunately, Peter's initial lack of concern about the effects of sun exposure is a typical attitude shared by many. People should take more action to prevent health problems caused by overexposure to the sun.

Delivered in the third person, the account works as an effective opening because of its human interest. People are interested in other people. Audience members may also relate personally to Peter's story.

A first person experience is the third type of illustration that can be used to begin a speech. Telling an interesting story about yourself that builds to a definite climax and ends with a statement of thesis and direction will gain the audience's attention. By revealing something about yourself, you may even develop a communal sense of "It happened to me, it could happen to you," or "We're all in this together." Here is Peter's introduction on the harmful effects of the sun written as a personal experience from the "I" point of view.

I remember my last day at the beach. I had my towel and bathing suit ready to go as I waited for my friends to pick me up. When they arrived, I shouted "Good-bye" to my mom. As I sprinted out the door, I heard her ask if I had taken sunscreen with me. I yelled back "yeah," knowing very well that I didn't even think about taking any. When I got to the beach, the sun was bright and hot. My friends and I enjoyed a wonderful day, but the next day I noticed that my shoulders really hurt. A bad sunburn I concluded. "It will go away," I said to myself. Eventually, the pain did go away, but I noticed a small mole forming on my shoulder. It grew larger and began to ooze. When I visited a dermatologist and he did a biopsy, it turned out to be a malignant melanoma, the most dangerous kind of skin cancer. It was removed surgically, but now my whole life has changed because I was foolish enough not to protect myself from the harmful effects of the sun. Unfortunately, my lack of concern is the attitude shared by many people, maybe even by you. I learned the hard way. People should take more action to prevent health problems caused by overexposure to the sun.

Another way to wake up the audience is to shock or startle them. Shocking statements in the opening lines may stimulate audience attention. Startling statements may also arouse curiosity, especially if the statements pertain personally, in some way, to audience members.

In the following introduction to a speech about the AIDS epidemic, Adam uses a statistic to relate the number of people involved in the epidemic to the students in his small community.

Think for a second about the size of our city, Highland Park: 40,000 inhabitants. 40,000—that's how many teenagers are infected with the HIV virus in New York City alone. The AIDS epidemic can affect any one of us, just as it has already affected the 40,000 teenagers in New York City. Teenagers like us are especially susceptible because of engaging in unprotected sex. Schools must increase their efforts to educate students about responsible sexual behavior and consequences.

Adam mentions a shocking statistic in his introduction and then relates that statistic to his specific audience. By relating the numbers to his audience, he arouses their curiosity about the topic. This introduction is just one step away from the shocker that asks audience members to look at their neighbors and realize that, statistically speaking, something dire will happen to some of them within a certain amount of time. For example, in an introduction to a "welcoming" speech at a major university, the speaker asked new students to look at those seated to their immediate right and left, telling them that "By the end of the second month, one of these people will no longer attend the university; one of you will have flunked out." This shocking statement attracted everyone's attention and was remembered, not only during the speech, but years later. The statement was startling, realistic, and definitely pertained to the specific audience!

Not as dramatic as a shocking statement, but in some situations effective in gaining attention, is the use of a quotation. People are interested in what others have to say on a given subject, particularly authorities or experts. Especially in formal situations, a quotation is a fine way to engage the audience and present the topic to be covered. In the following introduction to a speech on the quality of the nation's teachers, Taka uses an opening quotation from an authority, an author of a book on the subject. He then quickly moves into his thesis statement. This direct approach often works well in informative and persuasive speeches.

Rita Kramer, author of the book *Ed School Follies* said, "The single most important factor in an individual's education is his teachers. . .What we need if we are to touch the minds of children, rescue the public school system, and the democracy it should nourish, are inspiring teachers." If, in fact, Ms. Kramer's statements are true, then teachers are perhaps some of the most important people in a child's life, since they help to determine that child's future. Yet, many of our teachers are of low quality, and for that reason, our education system suffers. To improve our nation's public schools, we need to improve the quality of the teachers.

Outside of the classroom, you may be asked to give a speech on a special occasion. The speech can take the form of a tribute at a wedding or perhaps you need to write a political campaign speech. In speeches where the purpose of the presentation relates to an occasion, you may want to begin the speech by referring to the occasion. In the following example, Susan's introduction relates to the middle school graduation at which she delivered the speech.

The tin man, the cowardly lion, the scarecrow—by now these characters are all familiar to you. But what special meaning can they have for you at this important moment in your lives? Tonight, as you walk across this stage and move from one stage in your life to another, let's reflect on these characters from Oz to see how their experiences can provide advice and direction for high school.

In contrast to the body of the speech, which is typically written in outline form and delivered extemporaneously (prepared but conversationally), the introduction might be recorded word for word, exactly as you plan to deliver it. Because strong, confident delivery is essential to establish a positive first impression, you will want to deliver the opening lines exactly as you planned them. If the introduction goes smoothly, you will gain the confidence to you proceed with the rest of your speech.

PREPARING A STRONG CONCLUSION

The introduction and conclusion are the bookends that hold your speech together. Just as a strong introduction is crucial to capture your audience's attention, a strong conclusion will leave the audience with a positive impression of both you and your speech content. If the introduction provides the "grabber," the conclusion provides the "clincher" to the speech. Here are some suggestions for developing a forceful conclusion.

An effective conclusion brings the speech to an obvious end. Many inexperienced speakers use "thank you" as a conclusion. In some cases you may want to thank audience members for their attention; however, if you have done your job properly, the audience will know that your speech has ended without your expressing appreciation for listening.

Because the conclusion is one of the bookends that frames the speech, relating it back to either the content or the form of the introduction can be effective. Referring back to the introduction helps the audience to feel a sense of completion and an understanding of the full scope of your speech. Some conclusions look toward the future with a prediction, recommended course of action, promise, or hope. In the following conclusion from her speech at the middle school graduation, Susan combines *Wizard of Oz* references used in the introduction with a prediction.

> The scarecrow, the tin man, and the lion realized that all the ingredients they needed to achieve their dreams, they already possessed. And just like those

Ozian characters, if you realize the potential within you to expand your caring, your courage, and your academic prowess, you will undoubtedly walk your yellow brick road to success. As you cross this stage to begin your journey, I know that each of you will soon discover, in the most wonderful way possible, that there truly is no place like high school; there is no place like high school.

Good conclusions often summarize the major points emphasized in the speech body. This summary may take the form of a general restatement of the theme of the speech, or it may incorporate a listing of the major points of the speech body. A summary helps to give audience members a sense of completion as well as a final reminder of the significant elements of your speech. To keep the audience's visual attention focused until the very end of the speech, use an exhibit or visual aid. In the following conclusion from her speech "Biological Cloning: A Two-Way Mirror," Richenda combines a summary with a personal appeal and the use of a visual aid.

Biological cloning is definitely a two-sided mirror. Cloning cells of animals and humans could lead to finding cures for diseases such as AIDS and influenza, yet it could also lead to a more unethical society where people are used merely as twin body parts. Many other controversial questions arise on cloning humans, too, such as who has the right to determine which embryos should be cloned? I urge you to become a part of the majority of respondents in the *Time* magazine survey who questioned the morality of cloning. Because of the negative consequences of biological cloning, the only way we should be able to see a reflection of our unique selves is through one of these. [Richenda holds up a mirror facing the audience.]

Richenda used her conclusion to summarize the major point of her speech. However, her conclusion was especially effective because of the combination of elements: the restatement of major points, the visual aid, and the personal appeal, "I urge you. . ." The personal appeal reminds the audience of how the topic relates to them. It may also help them to respond to the message on an emotional level, as opposed to a purely intellectual level.

Because people often make decisions and take courses of action based on their feelings about things, and not on a logical analysis of a situation, an emotional appeal can be an especially effective way to conclude a speech. The emotional appeal may focus on sympathy for an individual's or a group's desperate plight, or the appeal may relate to general emotions such as patriotism, pride, or honor. An emotional appeal may break down barriers between the speaker and the audience.

Another way to continue to close the gap between you and the audience in the conclusion is the use of humor. If you can make your audience laugh, you will bring them closer to you and to the purpose of your speech. However, just as in the introduction, prepared humor may not always work according to plan. Be flexible and move right on if you don't get the laughter you desire.

In the following conclusion from his speech on the Chicago Cubs, Steve uses an emotional appeal for his final argument on why his audience should become Cubs fans. He also uses some tongue-in-cheek humor to keep his audience both guessing and focused. Finally, in this conclusion, Steve returns to his thesis, to eliminate doubt about the clarity of his message.

Now that I have explained to you why you should cheer on the Cubs, just remember this: Anybody can root for a winner such as the Yankees or the Braves, but it takes sheer guts, courage, and determination to root for the underdog, the Chicago Cubs. Long-suffering fans of the Cubs have lived through many a miserable season, but there have been winning years too—like 1908. It's this simple: True fans will always support the Cubs. The patriots fought for America; Cubs fans fight for the Cubs. The Cubs mean fun and excitement. They are a team rich in tradition. The Chicago Cubs: America's true team. Everyone should root for the Cubs.

In his conclusion, Steve asks for audience members to assume a general behavior or attitude. However, some speeches end effectively with calls or recommendations for specific action. If the speech relates to an issue or problem that can be addressed through the political process, it may end with the command, "Write your congressional representative today!" The following conclusion, from a demonstration speech on juggling, suggests, in concrete terms, what audience members should do.

> Juggling is a great recreational activity; it truly
> takes your mind off work and responsibility. After all,
> how else can you go crazy by getting three balls to
> jump around according to patterns? Everyone in this
> audience can learn to juggle quickly and easily. Just
> buy three balls and follow the steps described in this
> speech. Begin today!

Just as a story, example or illustration can be good devices to begin a speech, illustrations often make effective conclusions. Although you can strengthen the major points made in the body of your speech with examples, illustrations, and other types of verbal support, a final example or story in the conclusion may help to cement your thesis. The following conclusion comes from a speech on frivolous lawsuits. The speech body was filled with examples to make the case that frivolous lawsuits are becoming an extremely serious problem in today's courts. However, Bram used one final story in the conclusion for final reinforcement.

> Christopher Duffy stole a car from a parking lot
> and was killed in an accident while he was driving
> that stolen car. The estate of car thief Duffy

subsequently sued the proprietor of the parking lot for failing to prevent auto theft. Cases such as this one are clogging our court system. People who are just looking to make a quick buck through frivolous lawsuits must be stopped before the litigation explosion becomes a bomb that destroys our legal system.

Another way to reinforce your major point in the conclusion is to use a quotation. A strong quotation lends a sense of authority to the conclusion as well as giving it a definite finality, an ending "punch." In the following conclusion to his speech on the negative effects of exposure to the sun, Peter uses a simple, yet effective quotation. It summarizes the message of the speech and incorporates a little rhyme.

The problems caused by "The Dark Side of the Sun" continue to grow. We can't stop them, but you can prevent yourself from becoming a victim of unprotected sun exposure. By being careful and prepared, you can do yourself a lot of good. You can enjoy the sun and stay healthy. Just remember what Rosemary Ellis, a writer for the Atlantic City Press said, "If you want to keep the summer fun, don't get too much sun."

Your conclusion must be carefully prepared because it represents the last impression that you will be able to make on the audience. Therefore, just as with the introduction, you should write it out word for word and memorize it for optimal delivery. Memorization is important because you will want to plan your phrasing exactly for the final "punch," especially in the very last sentence of the speech.

Conclusion

Now that you are familiar with preparing the content, the "what" of the speech, you are ready to move on to the delivery, the "how" of the speech. But before you do, take a look at the following diagram which illustrates the steps involved in constructing a speech. If you have followed each step in preparing your content, you now need to focus your energies on the second half of effective public speaking: delivery.

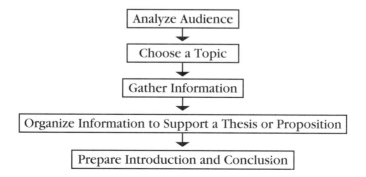

5

NONVERBAL COMMUNICATION

When you give an effective speech, a speech that works, you must attract and maintain your audience's attention. You accomplish this by saying something new, well organized and interesting and by presenting the message in an attention-sustaining manner. The way in which you present the message is called *delivery*. Without strong delivery, the best-prepared speech content will fall flat. Although well-organized, specific content is crucial to ensuring a successful speech, just as important to a speech's effectiveness is the delivery.

THE IMPORTANCE OF NONVERBAL COMMUNICATION

Delivery can be divided into two parts: verbal, the words you choose to use, and nonverbal, all the messages you convey in addition to or in place of words. Some experts believe that at least half of all real communication is nonverbal. (McCutcheon, p.78). Nonverbal communication can serve three functions in relation to verbal communication. It can augment or reinforce, contradict, or replace verbal communication. If your words and your nonverbal communication are conveying the same message, then you are augmenting your verbal message nonverbally. For example, if you say that something delights you and you have a big smile on your face, the receiver of your message can sense its sincerity.

Your nonverbal and verbal communication have worked together to strengthen the message. On the other hand, if you say that you are perfectly happy and comfortable, yet you are wringing your hands, your nonverbal message is contradicting your verbal communication. Perceptive communication receivers know that when the nonverbal and verbal messages contradict each other, the nonverbal communication almost always conveys the true message. Therefore, what someone conveys nonverbally can cancel out a verbal message.

In addition to canceling a verbal message, nonverbal communication can replace words. For example, if you want to ask for the audience's attention, instead of saying, "May I please have your attention?", you might just raise your hand and wait for them to get the signal, or you might stand silently in front of the room and wait. Your raised hand and/or silence can be more effective in sending the message than words could be.

Because of the presence and power of nonverbal communication, any time we interact with other people, whether or not we are in a public speaking situation, we are always communicating. If you want to deliver a truly effective speech, you will need to think of how you can use nonverbal communication to augment or strengthen your message. Sometimes aspects of nonverbal communication are referred to as *body language*. Body language and the language of words serve a common function together: They help us to communicate. When giving a speech, you need to think of how you will use these elements together to get your message across in the manner that you want to convey it.

MAKING NONVERBAL COMMUNICATION WORK FOR YOU

Before you give a speech, one of the first things to consider is the space in which you will be speaking. You need to "make friends with the room." How large is it? Where will most of the audience members be seated? In what configuration will they sit? Rows? Semicircle? Where and how will you position yourself? Will you stand behind a lectern or on a podium, or will you have the freedom to move around a bit? Physical movement is a good strategy for holding the audience's attention because action creates and holds visual focus. However, the action must be limited and purposeful or else it can become distracting and detract from the strength of your message.

Probably the most important moment of your speech is the walk to the front of the room where you will address the audience. That walk can set the tone for your entire speech. You can give the audience the impression that you are excited and prepared to give the speech, or you can appear underconfident and unsure about what you are about to do. If you walk to the front of the room with an air of confidence and conviction, not only will you appear eager to deliver your speech, but you will create a positive impression and make the audience eager to listen to you.

Because you will probably not be speaking as you walk to the podium, what you convey about yourself and your message, the first impression of your speech, will be communicated nonverbally. As you approach the place from which you will speak, you will likely be nervous; you may even feel a little queasy. Some people call this sensation "butterflies in the stomach." You may feel a little shaky because your body is responding to a stress situation. You are experiencing a *psychosomatic* reaction: your mind and body are connected and are working together to handle a challenging condition. These feelings are completely normal; in fact, they can actually help you to deliver an excellent speech.

How can extreme nervousness, even queasiness help you to give a good speech? The fear that you have of public speaking registers in your brain. The brain then signals the adrenal glands to release a hormone called *adrenalin*. That adrenalin gives you the extra energy that you need to respond to a challenge. Channeled properly the extra energy adrenaline causes can make your speech appear lively and enthusiastic.

Therefore, as you walk to the front of the room, take a few deep breaths to control your tension. No matter how you feel inside, walk in a determined, confident manner to the lectern, with your shoulders back and head high. When you reach the front of the room, pause for a few seconds to make sure that you have everyone's visual attention. After you have glanced around the room and looked directly into as many faces as possible, you can begin to speak.

The two most obvious types of nonverbal communication during a speech are *eye contact*, how you look at audience members, and *gestures*, the use of hand movements. Eye contact is critical to establishing and maintaining good communication between you and your audience. Even before you speak, you should try to look directly into as many eyes as you can. Hold each individual's gaze for a second or two and then move on to another. In most speaking situations, you will be close enough to listeners to see their eyes. If you are speaking to a few thousand people at a graduation or other large ceremony, holding individual eye contact will be difficult. In this case, try to look in the direction of as many individual faces as you can.

Eye contact is extremely important in establishing and maintaining a connection with your audience. However, it is only one form of nonverbal communication. Another is sometimes called *paralanguage*. Paralanguage is all vocal, but not verbal communication. In addition to tone of voice, emphasis, force, pausing, sighing, laughing and quivering, paralanguage includes vocalized pauses such as "um," "uh," "well," and "you know." Use of paralanguage can help to indicate how you feel about speaking. If you are confident and feel that you know your content, your vocal delivery may be forceful and smooth. On the other hand, if remembering even the first line of your introduction is a struggle, then vocalized pauses such as "um," "uh," and "you know" will reveal your discomfort with the speech. Remember, if you appear uncomfortable, your audience will also feel uneasy. Use paralanguage and all types of nonverbal communication to add to everyone's sense of comfort and confidence.

In addition to eye contact and paralanguage, nonverbal communication includes the use of gestures to replace or complement words. For example, if you list items in a speech, you may want to hold up fingers to signify numbers. You may want to use your hands to show acceptance or giving (palms up) or rejection or stopping (palms down). The thumbs-up expression means something positive and, of course, thumbs-down means just the opposite. You may also use gestures to help clarify concepts such as size or shape.

Generally speaking, to use gestures effectively to enhance verbal communication, avoid planning too carefully which gestures you will use at various points in a speech. You should begin speaking with your hands at your sides and concentrate solely on the message you are sending. If you become truly involved with communicating that message, your hands will probably just move by themselves, without your conscious planning. For example, if you become very emphatic about a point, you may clench your fist. Perhaps you will make an emotional appeal with a hand gesture toward the audience.

Gestures will spring naturally from the strength of your message. If they are not predetermined, they will look natural and will add to communication, as opposed to detracting from communication. The fact that we unconsciously "talk" with our hands is another aspect of the psycho-somatic element of communication. Our minds and bodies are connected and working together to help us get our messages across to others.

Occasionally, you may be asked to speak to a large audience in a formal situation where you stand on a podium behind a lectern and use a microphone to amplify your voice. For most presentations, such as those in classroom situations, you will speak to a group of approximately twenty-five individuals and you may not have to use a lectern or speaking stand for notes. To maximize the nonverbal aspect of your delivery, try not to be tied to a lectern. If you move with purpose as you speak, you will enhance your delivery. Movement demands attention; if you combine it with the use of physical properties, audience members will have the opportunity not only to *listen*, but to *see*.

Moving with purpose means that you do not have to stand absolutely still during a speech. Take a few steps at strategic moments. For example, as you move through your speech from one section to another, you may want to take a few steps to help indicate the transition through the use of movement and space. What you do not want to do is to sway or step about aimlessly and often. Movement must be limited and natural to add to and not distract from the meaning of the speech.

Using space to maximize delivery can help to make your message more effective. Depending on what kind of presentation you're giving, you may want to alter the physical space. Because audience members do not expect a speaker to invade personal or listening space, walking toward certain individuals or even touching them in some way will definitely command attention.

To make sure that you are free to move, use notes—but use them purposefully and sparingly. On a 3 x 5 inch note card, jotting down a few words to help you to remember major points, statistics, and quotations can facilitate smooth delivery. A note card is small and has some weight so that it is an efficient and nondistracting way to provide help with verbal content.

Both tactile communication (touching) and spatial communication (use of space) can help to make your message unforgettable. For example, if your speech covers how to train a dog and you bring in a real dog, you may want to ask listeners to arrange their chairs in a large semicircle so that everyone can easily see the dog and so that the dog has enough space to perform with its trainer. For a speech on how to clean a bedroom, you may want to move the furniture so that the room more closely resembles a bedroom. During a speech on etiquette, you may want to shake selected audience members' hands to demonstrate proper form. In most cases, you do not need to think of the space in the front of the room behind the lectern as the only space you can use when giving a speech. Think ahead about how you can change the space to fit your communication needs and then use the space to your best advantage.

THE DEMONSTRATION SPEECH: USING VISUAL AIDS

Nonverbal communication is particularly important to the success of the *demonstration speech*, wherein the speaker must describe and show a process to the audience. A demonstration speech can be a great deal of fun to deliver if you are thoroughly familiar with and enjoy both showing and telling about the topic. Demonstration speeches, by their very nature, can also lessen the natural anxiety that you experience during a speech. Because you are showing something, your body is involved in purposeful action. Just holding and manipulating an object can help you to relax because you have something to do with your hands. The extra surge of energy that you feel during a presentation can be channeled and put to good use.

Part of making a demonstration speech successful is knowing how to use visual aids effectively. Important tools in communication, visual aids can help to clarify points and impress listeners while helping them to remember your verbal content. For example, if you were trying to get somewhere, imagine following only verbal directions: To get to the beach from the highway, go north to the Clavey Road exit, turn right on Clavey Road to Green Bay Road, left on Green Bay to Roger Williams Road, right on Roger Williams (past the railroad crossing) to Sheridan Road, right on Sheridan for one block to 800 Sheridan Road on the right and the beach entrance on the left.

Now see if you can visualize how to get to the beach if you are listening to the verbal directions while the speaker provides the following diagram.

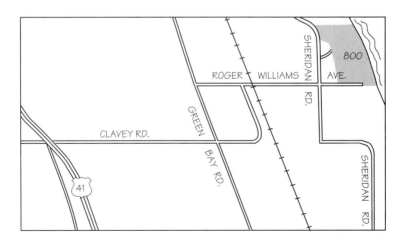

For most people, being able to see a diagram or map makes finding the destination much more likely. Because words alone are not always up to the task of communicating fully, nonverbal communication in the form of a sketch or diagram can help you to show, as well as tell your message in a clear, precise way.

To ensure that your visual aids really do help you to communicate, you need to think about how to prepare and use them purposefully. First, make sure that all of your audience can see and appreciate each aid. This means that your drawings or objects must be large enough and clear enough for everyone to see. If you are demonstrating a process, you may have to create a visual aid that shows aspects of the process in exaggerated size. For example, if your speech covers how to produce hair wraps, you should create large diagrams showing the steps of the process. Pieces of thread and fine finger movements are just too small to be seen and appreciated by twenty-five people at once.

Time the introduction and use of the visual aids carefully. Before you begin the speech, make sure that the physical objects are easily accessible to you and ready to use. Think about the best ways for your visual aids to enhance your verbal content. In most cases, you will not want to display all of your visual aids at once. You may create suspense by saving an aid for just the right moment.

Tom, for example, gave a demonstration speech on the care and feeding of his pet. He brought a pillowcase to the front of the room and placed it in an inconspicuous location. He introduced his speech with the following:

Some people say that a dog is "man's best friend." That may be true for some people, but I think that I have found a pet that is loyal, fun to play with, and whose care is not terribly difficult. He is one of my best friends. I'd like to introduce you to Joey.

As he spoke the name "Joey," Tom held up the pillowcase, and pulled out his best friend—a snake. Throughout the rest of the speech, Joey slithered around Tom's neck as Tom explained how to feed and take care of Joey. Tom showed and told about why Joey made such a good pet.

The timing of Tom's introduction of his visual aid—Joey—maximized its effectiveness. Because Tom did not show the snake at the beginning, but instead kept his audience in suspense, his listeners were curious about exactly who and what the pet could be. Additionally, because the pet was on display for the body of the speech, the audience's attention was riveted on Tom and his snake. Finally, at the conclusion of the speech, Tom brought out the pillowcase and put Joey away. Because of the way he used the pillowcase in the introduction, showing it again provided an effective visual conclusion to the speech.

Timing the use of a visual aid is indeed crucial to its effectiveness. You should introduce an object at the moment when it will best serve the needs of the message. If you bring out the object at just the right moment, you will be able to maximize visual suspense. If you introduce it too early, you may detract from your message. If you bring it out too late, it may be anticlimactic. When you are finished showing the visual aid, put it away so that it doesn't detract from the rest of your speech. Also, avoid circulating objects in the audience during the speech. Doing so while you are speaking is a sure way to cause distraction, and perhaps even audience conversation while you are talking.

If you demonstrate a process, you will receive audience feedback. If that feedback indicates confusion, you may have to repeat parts of the demonstration. If you will not exceed your allotted time limit by doing so, repeating parts of a process is perfectly acceptable but be careful: Too much repetition can result in boredom.

Remember, no matter how you feel about the quality of your visual aids, never apologize for them. Just as you should act confidently about other aspects of your speech, you should appear to be proud of the quality of your visual aids as communication tools. Comments such as, "I'm sorry, I'm not a very good artist" will not contribute to the effectiveness of your message. If you have prepared your visual aids carefully in advance, assume that they are enhancing your verbal content and display them proudly.

COMBINING SHOWING AND TELLING

One of the most challenging parts of giving a demonstration speech is to remember to tell as you show. Nothing is more boring than listening to a "how-to" speech on food preparation and watching someone stir or mix in silence for a few minutes. When you show a process, you should prepare enough new, specific verbal content to maintain a running commentary during the demonstration. Therefore, just as you would for an informative, personal experience, or persuasive speech, you should prepare an outline that contains the bulk of your verbal content.

The outline should set forth the thesis statement that defines your topic and reveals your attitude about it. It should also contain the three major parts of a speech: introduction, body, and conclusion. The body of the speech should explain what will be demonstrated. It should also provide information about how the demonstration will work. You might include a list of the steps in the process as well as background information about the topic or the process.

From the following outline two students, Bram and Scott, will inform their audience about the various methods of juggling in a seven-minute demonstration speech. To enhance the speech, they plan to show various techniques of juggling. In this outline, they wrote out their introduction and conclusion word for word. The body of the outline is in sentence form to ensure that they have thought the concepts through carefully.

Introduction:

A book entitled *Juggling for the Complete Klutz* described juggling as "one form of insanity we feel everyone has the right to experience." The insanity comes in many stages. The first and longest part of the insanity is spending a month trying to get three balls to jump around in your hands. After you master the basic process, you reach the next stage of insanity when you try to get the three balls to jump around in different

ways. With the insanity comes fun and challenge.
Juggling is a fun and easy hobby after you master
the basics.

Body:

I. Juggling is a beneficial hobby that has been
    practiced for thousands of years.

    A. Juggling has been an art form for a
    long time.

        1. Juggling can be found in written records
    of early Egyptian and surrounding
    ancient civilizations.

        2. Records show that people have been
    juggling for over 4,000 years.

    B. Juggling is physically and mentally
    helpful.

        1. Juggling is a mental exercise.

            a. You can learn to use the right side
    of your brain which may not be used
    much during the day.

            b. Juggling helps you relax and
    loosens tension.

            c. Juggling has been prescribed by
    doctors to relieve stress.

        2. Juggling can help strengthen the body.

            a. It can help build muscles in the
    upper body.

        b. It can also improve hand-eye
           coordination.
 II. An enjoyable aspect of juggling is that you can
     juggle with a great variety of objects.
     A. Good juggling objects meet a
         few requirements.
         1. They have to fit comfortably in
             your hand.
         2. They have to weigh the right amount.
            a. They have to weigh enough so that
               they don't float in the air
               when thrown.
            b. They can't be so heavy that they are
               impossible to throw.
     B. Beanbags are the most basic juggling items.
         1. Because they are easy to grasp,
             they are the perfect items for
             beginning jugglers.
         2. They are inexpensive and easy to find.
     C. Other items are fun to juggle as you become
         proficient.
         1. You can juggle beanbags in shapes of
             other objects, such as animals.
         2. You can juggle fresh produce, which is
             easily obtainable at the market.

       3. You can juggle clubs.

       4. If you become an expert, you can juggle dangerous items such as knives or lit torches.

III. Juggling is an easy process if you practice the four simple steps.

  A. The first step is called the drop.

     1. Throw the balls up in the air and let them fall to the ground.

     2. Pick them up and repeat the process.

     3. Get used to the feeling because when you are learning it happens naturally.

  B. The second step is throwing one ball back and forth between your two hands.

     1. Get comfortable with throwing the ball back and forth.

     2. Make sure the ball is under control all the time while you are throwing it.

  C. The next step is called an exchange.

     1. Throw the ball in your right hand to the left hand, and while the first ball is in the air throw the second ball, which is in your left hand up and under the first ball,

to your right hand. Then catch the
balls as they come to your hands.

    2. You need to be in control of the balls
during the exchange.

    3. Your throws have to be on target
to your hands to move on to the
next step.

  D. The final step is juggling.

    1. You begin with two balls in your right
hand and one in your left.

    2. You do an exchange with one ball from
both hands, then before you catch the
second ball, you throw the third ball
under the second ball.

    3. You continue to throw and catch balls
in this manner.

IV. After you practice and master the basic
juggling process, you will be ready to try
complex juggling tricks.

  A. "Double tosses" are challenging but
versatile tricks.

    1. You throw one ball in each hand to the
opposite hand; then, when you are about

to catch the two balls, you throw the
third one in between the other
two and begin juggling.

  2. This pattern can be used to start
juggling or can be executed
while juggling.

B. "Under the leg" is an exciting trick.

  1. You simply throw the ball under your
leg while juggling, and you recover and
continue juggling.

  2. "Under the leg" has many variations,
such as throwing the ball behind your
back or neck.

C. "Elevators" is a two-in-one trick.

  1. Juggle two balls in your right hand, but
instead of juggling in a circular
pattern, throw the balls
vertically, next to each other.

  2. In the other hand, throw the remaining
ball up and catch it

Conclusion:

Juggling is a unique hobby. With a little
practice, you can master basic patterns and move on
to more difficult tricks. Only this hobby lets you

spend your time going crazy, trying to get three balls to jump around in different patterns. And insanity means not being able to stop your craziness. Like my partner and me, after you get a taste of how much fun juggling is, you won't ever be able to stop.

In this speech, Bram and Scott used visual aids to their utmost advantage as they described and demonstrated a process. Their nonverbal communication augmented what they had to say. Verbal and nonverbal communication worked together to deliver a message.

SELECTING A DEMONSTRATION SPEECH TOPIC

In choosing a topic for a demonstration speech, think about a process that you would like to demonstrate, something that the audience would be interested in and that would be new to them. Sample topics include:

1. How to sculpt with soap
2. How to apply a cast
3. How to pack a suitcase properly
4. How to construct a piñata
5. How to apply clown makeup
6. How to make puppets
7. How to construct a skateboard or the techniques of skateboarding
8. How to make figures through paper folding (the Japanese art of origami)
9. How to change a bicycle tire
10. How to do magic tricks

Conclusion

A demonstration speech is one way to combine the use of physical materials and nonverbal communication with verbal communication to get a message across, but effective nonverbal communication is critical in any excellent speech. In the next chapter, you will learn about the partner of nonverbal communication in strong speaking—effective vocal communication.

6

YOUR VOICE AS A TOOL

CHAPTER

Your voice is the basic instrument of speaking, and how you use it can determine the difference between an effective and an ineffective presentation. The sound of your voice, by itself, communicates something important about you and is one of your most distinctive, personal characteristics. The way your voice sounds presents an impression of you to others. The sound of your voice is often termed *vocal quality*. To use your voice, the instrument of speech, to its fullest advantage, and to enhance your speaking capabilities, you need to know how your body produces both your voice and speech.

PRODUCING YOUR VOICE

You know that your voice has a distinctive quality to it, a quality that others can recognize over the phone after you have spoken just a word or two. Your voice is produced by a mechanism that does what all sound producing instruments do—vibrate. The air that you take in and breathe out creates the source of energy that produces the sound that eventually becomes your voice. As you inhale, the *diaphragm,* a powerful muscle between the chest and the abdomen, contracts and flattens. The ribs move up and out to increase the size of the chest cavity. When you exhale, the diaphragm pushes upward and helps to drive air out of the lungs. This air moves through the *trachea* (windpipe) and past the *larynx* (voice box) where sound is produced. If you choose to speak, the air moving up through the trachea also moves through the *vocal folds,* causing them to vibrate. This vibration creates a sound that eventually becomes your voice.

The initial sound is thin and probably not terribly pleasing. However, the sound waves pass through a number of cavities, called *resonators.* As the sound waves become amplified, these resonators help your voice to sound rich and full. The resonators are the larynx itself, the *pharynx* (the back of the throat), the nose, and the mouth. If all of the resonators are in good shape, your voice is most likely rich, full, and somewhat pleasing. However, an obstruction, growth, or other problem in one of the resonators will affect your vocal quality. For example, if you have a bad cold and your nose is stuffed up, you won't be able to inhale or exhale properly through your nose. Because you will have limited nasal resonance, the quality of your voice will change to a less pleasing, *denasal* sound. If you have a growth in a resonator, your voice may take on a harsh or scratchy sound. If you have a major vocal quality problem, the cause is most likely medical and should be treated by a doctor.

CREATING SPEECH

Voice becomes speech through *articulators,* the instruments that shape sound into words. The articulators are the teeth, lips, tongue, and *palate* (the roof of the mouth). If you use the articulators to shape vowel and consonant sounds correctly, then your speech should be intelligible and clear. However, if one of your articulators changes in shape or is not working correctly, clear speech will be difficult. For example, if a front tooth is missing, making the *s* sound properly is hard to do. Often, a *th* sound will be substituted. When people get braces on their teeth, they need to compensate for the extra weight and texture on their teeth to articulate properly. For someone who has an injured lip, making the *p* and *b* sounds correctly will be difficult. Therefore, to produce the clearest speech possible, the articulators must be in good working order and you must use them properly. This means that while giving a speech, you should open your mouth and make all the sounds distinctly. If you speak with a clenched jaw or teeth, your message will be hard to decipher.

In addition to good articulation, you must have proper pronunciation for a speech to be clear and easy to understand. This means that you should know how to say the various vowel and consonant sounds in words and know where the accented syllables should be. During a speech, you want the audience to concentrate on the message you are presenting; you do *not* want them distracted by your errors. And make no mistake about this: mispronunciations are distracting. Sometimes a mispronunciation will merely confuse the audience; sometimes audience members will become distracted by it and will become skeptical about how knowledgeable the speaker really is. If you know in advance that you will be using technical or new (to you) vocabulary during a speech, consult the dictionary. Look up and practice the correct pronunciations before you give the speech. We all have much greater reading vocabularies than spoken ones. We can recognize a word and can tell what it means in the context of a reading passage. However, we may not know how to say the word out loud. To maximize your effectiveness, make sure that you articulate each sound properly and pronounce each word correctly. Do not embarrass yourself or confuse your audience by placing the emphasis on the wrong syllable.

VARYING YOUR VOICE TO EXPRESS MEANING

One of the most important ways to use your voice effectively during a speech is to vary it, both for emphasis and to help make your meaning clear. The three most common types of vocal variety are pitch, rate, and volume. *Pitch* is how high or low your voice is on a musical scale. *Rate* is how quickly or slowly you speak. *Volume* is how loudly or softly you speak. You have probably heard the term monotone. If you speak in a *monotone,* you are speaking with primarily one pitch and volume. The word *monotone* definitely connotes *boring.* To keep your speech interesting, you must vary your voice by changing its pitch, rate and volume.

You can change pitch in one of two ways. Changing pitch during an utterance, while you are saying a syllable or making a sound, is called an *inflection*. If your voice goes up in pitch, you have a rising inflection. If your voice goes down in pitch, you have a falling inflection. You can also move your pitch both up and down in a single utterance, creating a combination: pitch will both rise and fall during one syllable. If you change pitch in between syllables or words, you have made a pitch shift. The actual change occurs after a millisecond of silence. Varying pitch is extremely important to keep your audience engaged and to reinforce your message.

Pitch variety carries messages of its own. For example, a rising inflection can express surprise, uncertainty, or unfinished business. A falling inflection can suggest finality, sincerity, or conviction. The combined inflection can signify doubt, confusion or sarcasm. You use pitch variety naturally when you speak informally, during a conversation. During a speech, just as you must amplify conversational volume, you may want to exaggerate pitch variety to make sure that your message is clear.

Rate variety is also important in maintaining your audience's attention. Generally, you will want to speak at a brisk pace, yet not so brisk that the audience has a difficult time following you. You may want to slow down to reinforce the major points of your speech, emphasize a thesis statement, or build suspense. The use of *pause*, or a short, temporary silence, is part of rate variety. If not overused, it can help to maintain attention and emphasize major points. It can also help to build suspense.

The use of pause can be significant in making your meaning clear. However, you will want to use silence only to help transmit meaning, not because you have run out of breath. If you find that you have to stop to take breaths in the middle of phrases, you may want to try a few breathing exercises. Remember that the diaphragm, the muscle that separates the chest cavity from the abdominal cavity, should push out when you breathe in to expand the cavity which you will fill with air. Try this series of exercises: place your hand immediately below the rib cage. That is where the diaphragm is located. Now take a deep breath and make sure that the diaphragm is pushing out, expanding the cavity, as you inhale. Exhale as slowly as you can, feeling the diaphragm push in. Because you can only speak while you are exhaling, you need to take in as much air as possible and exhale slowly so as not to run out of breath while you are speaking. If you practice taking in large breaths while pushing your diaphragm out and then exhaling slowly, your breath control should increase.

Finally, volume variety serves to hold an audience's attention and reinforce your message. By varying your volume, you strengthen the force of your message. Novice speakers sometimes think that their most important points have to be spoken the loudest; that they should build to a climax in a speech and then speak loudly once there. A crescendo in volume can be helpful for emphasis, but so can a sudden drop in volume. If your voice is quite loud and then you drop it at a crucial point to just above an audible whisper, your audience may strain to hear you, but the moment will be dramatic. Whether you choose to increase or lower your volume at strategic points in your speech, you must vary it to attract and hold your audience's interest.

UNDERSTANDING AND INTERPRETING LITERATURE

In all speeches, whether extemporaneous, memorized, manuscript, or impromptu, you must use your voice effectively as the primary instrument of communication. However, the focus on your voice as a communication tool must be particularly keen in the type of speech known as an *oral interpretation of literature*. In an oral interpretation, you share someone else's words with the audience using your voice and, sometimes, limited gestures. Such sharing is done in an expressive and meaningful way, so that the audience gets more out of listening to you just once than they would if they had read and reread the text. To give an oral interpretation of literature, as opposed to an oral reading, you must understand the literature well, and you must prepare a way to use your voice and face to communicate your understanding to the audience.

The first step in preparing an oral interpretation is to choose a selection that interests you. You will probably have certain parameters to guide you in your choice. You may be asked to interpret nonfiction, such as someone else's speech or a persuasive essay in a newspaper column. This kind of interpretation is often called *oratorical declamation.* You may be asked to comment on a prose fiction selection from a short story or novel, or you may be asked to analyze a poem. In any case, you will need to share your feelings about the piece, combined with what you believe to be the author's original intention, through the power of your voice.

How do you know the author's original intention? You can only guess, but the guess can be an educated one if you conduct a literary analysis. In other words, take the piece and break it down into its various components to acquire a solid understanding of it. After you finish analyzing the piece, you will have a better sense of its elements and of the messages the author meant to convey. You can then add your own interpretation to your analysis.

In a work of nonfiction, you will need to analyze the form. At what point is the thesis stated and why? In what ways does the author build to a climax or high point? Specifically, how does the author use language to reinforce the point? What do the sentences look like? Are they long? Short? How does the author vary sentence patterns? How does the author weave in quotations? Do any patterns emerge?

Whether analyzing nonfiction, prose fiction or poetry, you should look for *figurative* language, language that can make you see comparisons in new ways. Figures of speech include *allusions,* when an author makes a reference to a piece of knowledge not actually mentioned. For example, an author might state, "He was another Huck," alluding to the adventurous spirit of Mark Twain's *Huckleberry Finn.*

A *simile* is another example of figurative language typically used by good authors. A simile is an indirect comparison of one thing to another, using the words *like* or *as.* For example, an author might observe that, "Jose was so hungry that he growled like a lion." Unlike simile, *metaphor* is a comparison in which an author equates one thing directly with another, as in "Jose was a hungry lion." Authors use figurative language, such as similes or metaphors, to help intensify meaning.

Although writers use many techniques to make language vivid and expressive, two of the most common are *onomatopoeia* and *alliteration*. Onomatopoeia occurs when the pronunciation of a word echoes its meaning. Examples include the *buzz* of a bee or the *bang* of a gun. Alliteration means the repetition of an initial consonant sound in close succession, as in "Peter Piper picked a peck of pickled peppers," or "the fickle finger of fate."

In addition to noticing particularly expressive language, you need to think about the setting of a piece, when and where it takes place. You will also need to analyze its form and structure. Does the story take place in episodes, flashbacks (told from the present into the past) or chronologically, in the order of time?

For fiction selections, consider the point of view from which the story is told. Who is the narrator? Typically, stories are told from either an omniscient or first person point of view. The omniscient narrator knows everything and can move anywhere at any time. This narrator can also see into the minds and hearts of all of the characters and may know things about the characters that they themselves do not know. A first person narrator is limited to personal observation. This type of narrator is often an active character as well as an observer, and takes part in the development of the plot.

In a prose fiction analysis, you will need to consider the *plot*—the sequence of events in the story. The plot includes what happens, why, and to whom. It generally builds up to a climax (the peak or turning point of the structural and emotional content) and then works through to the denouement, or the solution or outcome of the story.

In addition to the plot, you will need to think about the major characters. Who are they? How old are they? What motivates their behavior? What is the basis for their emotions? Their hopes? Their fears? What makes them proud?

The mood of the piece is another important element in a literary analysis. The *mood* is the emotional attitude or feeling of a piece. Is it sad, happy, somber, depressing, light, humorous? Is there more than one mood to the piece? How do you know? What clues can you find in the language?

Finally, in any literary analysis you will need to identify the *theme* of the piece. What is the message? What point does the author seem to be making about life and the world?

SHARING LITERARY MEANING THROUGH ORAL INTERPRETATION

After you complete the analysis, you are ready to begin an oral interpretation. In some cases, you will need to prepare a *cutting,* an excerpt from a short story, novel, speech, or essay. If you must prepare a cutting, identify the climax of the piece or of a section of the piece and work backward. What parts of the description or dialogue can you omit and still tell the story? How can your cutting have a beginning, middle, and end to it?

In some cases, you will be able to present an oral interpretation of an entire piece of literature. The following poem, by Robert Frost, is a complete piece. Using the elements defined in the preceding pages, how would you analyze the poem? Read the poem a few times to determine its meaning. How did Frost use language to get his message across? If you were delivering this poem, where would you pause? Where would you raise or lower your voice in pitch or volume? In what ways would you vary rate? How does the rhythm of the language also contribute to the meaning?

"Out, Out—"

The buzz saw snarled and rattled in the yard	1
And made dust and dropped stove-length sticks of wood,	
Sweet-scented stuff when the breeze drew across it.	
And from there those that lifted eyes could count	
Five mountain ranges one behind the other	5
Under the sunset far into Vermont	
And the saw snarled and rattled, snarled and rattled,	
As it ran light, or had to bear a load.	
And nothing happened: day was all but done.	
Call it a day, I wish they might have said	10
To please the boy by giving him the half hour	
That a boy counts so much when saved from work.	
His sister stood beside them in her apron	
To tell them "Supper." At the word, the saw,	
As if to prove that saws knew what supper meant,	15
Leaped out at the boy's hand, or seemed to leap—	

He must have given the hand. However it was,
Neither refused the meeting. But the hand!
The boy's first outcry was a rueful laugh,
As he swung toward them holding up the hand,   20
Half in appeal, but half as if to keep
The life from spilling. Then the boy saw all—
Since he was old enough to know, big boy
Doing a man's work, though a child at heart—
He saw all spoiled. "Don't let him cut my hand off— 25
The doctor, when he comes. Don't let him sister!"
So. But the hand was gone already.
The doctor put him in the dark of ether.
He lay and puffed his lips out with his breath.
And then—the watcher at his pulse took fright.   30
No one believed. They listened at his heart.
Little—less—nothing!—and that ended it.
No more to build on there. And they, since they
Were not the one dead, turned to their affairs.

This poem tells a story. What is the mood of the story? Clearly, it is not light and happy. What is the climax of the story? How does the author use both onomatopoeia and alliteration to help advance the mood and plot? If you were giving an oral interpretation, what would you do with your voice to emphasize the "snarl" and "rattle" of the saw? Slowing your rate for "Sweet-scented stuff" might help the listener to picture what you were saying. The repetition of the initial *s* could even sound "sweet."

In lines 25 and 26, "Don't let him cut my hand off—. . . Don't let him sister!" would you vary volume to build intensity? Would you raise or lower it, or perhaps use a combination? How would you change pitch to bring out the desperate emotion in the words? In line 27, the word "So" is followed by a period. Why? How would you use pause there?

What are the messages of the poem? Assuming that one of them might be that no matter what tragedy hits us, life goes on, how could you convey this message through your voice in the last two lines?

"Out, Out—" can be viewed as an extremely powerful poem. These are just some of the questions that you would have to answer for yourself before you shared the meaning of the literature in a personal, yet powerful, way.

Here are some suggestions for using vocal variety to impart the meaning of this poem. These techniques can be used to interpret other pieces of poetry, and for prose as well.

"Out, Out—"
The **buzz** saw **snarled** and **rattled** in the yard　　1

Buzz, snarl *and* rattle *are all onomatopoeic words
—emphasize the buzzing, snarling and rattling
as you read*

And made dust // and dropped stove-length
sticks of wood, *[//=pause for emphasis]*
Sweet-scented stuff when the breeze drew across it.
*Emphasize the initial sounds of these three
alliterative words*

And from there those that lifted eyes could count
Five mountain ranges one behind the other　　5
Under the sunset far into Vermont //
pause after reading slowly and sweetly

And the saw snarled and rattled, snarled and rattled,
*Change tone, read harshly to exaggerate
onomatopoeia and repetition*

As it ran light, or had to bear a load.
And nothing happened: // day was all but done.
Call it a day, I wish they **might** have said　　10
raise pitch and volume to show anger and regret

To please the boy by giving him the half hour

That a boy counts so much when saved from work.

Raise pitch and volume to show boy's feelings

His sister stood beside them in her apron

To tell them **"Supper."** // At the word, the saw,

call the word and then pause for change in tone

As if to prove that saws knew what supper meant, 15

Leaped out at the boy's hand, or seemed to leap—

He must have given the hand. However it was,

Read rapidly to illustrate the speed of
the incident

Neither refused the meeting.

Read slowly and quietly to illustrate horror.

But the hand!

Lower pitch and volume to emphasize further
the horror.

The boy's first outcry was a rueful laugh,

As he swung toward them holding up the hand,   20

Half in appeal, // but half as if to keep

The life from spilling. Then the boy saw all—

Since he was old enough to know, big boy

Doing a man's work, though a child at heart—

He saw all spoiled.

Lower pitch, volume and slow rate to express realization.

"Don't let him cut my hand off—   25

The doctor, when he comes. Don't let

him sister!"

Raise pitch and volume to a frantic cry

So.

Lower volume and pitch to express resignation

But the hand was gone already. //

He lay and puffed his lips out with his breath.

And then—the watcher at his pulse took fright.   30

No one believed. They listened at his heart.

Little—//less—//nothing!—//and that ended it.

No more to build on there. //And **they,** since **they**

Were **not** the one dead,

Raise pitch and volume to emphasize change of focus

turned to their **affairs**.

Lower pitch and volume to show finality.

Conclusion

Through oral interpretation, and by understanding your voice and using it to transmit meaning, you can become a truly effective communicator. Now that you know how to use vocal and nonverbal communication techniques to enhance your delivery, you are ready for one of the greatest challenges of public speaking—persuasion.

7

CHAPTER

THE ART OF EFFECTIVE PERSUASION

Some believe that every speech or presentation is essentially persuasive in nature. At the very least, you have to convince your audience that they want to listen to you. However, two types of speeches are more obviously persuasive than others: the *move-to-action speech,* in which the goal is to motivate audience members to do something, and the *speech to convince,* designed to prove that a problem or condition exists or can be solved in a certain way.

MOVING OTHERS TO ACTION THROUGH PERSUASION

A move-to-action speech often takes the form of a selling speech, such as a television commercial, intended to motivate the audience to buy something. Because many advertised products and services are not essential to our basic needs (food, shelter, sleep, and so on) people who want to motivate others to buy must appeal to human nature and emotions. When you watch commercials on television, what kinds of appeals do you see?

Some of the typical appeals involve image advertising, which associates a product with attractive people, animals, or scenery. For example, alcoholic beverages are often advertised being consumed by beautiful people at parties or in romantic situations. Theoretically, the viewer should identify with the situation, want to be part of such a pleasant image, and buy the product. Similar to image advertising is the testimony of a well-known person or authority who acts as the spokesperson for a product or company.

Sometimes you will have to show something to move your audience to action. In the case of a selling speech, you may have to demonstrate the product as you talk about it, the time-honored presentation format for vacuum cleaner salespeople. A message that has visual or auditory appeal might help to sell a product. For example, an animated message or a peppy jingle might help persuade audience members to action.

Finally, appeals to the emotions can be quite persuasive. If your message elicits guilt, fear, shame, pride, or pleasure you may be able to reach your audience. Additionally, if you can provoke laughter, you may break down resistance to your message and move your audience to action.

This original television commercial was written by Debbie, a high school student. Debbie incorporated visual aids in this commercial, and her message was videotaped. Her classmates and teacher found this commercial to be particularly effective in moving the audience to action. Can you tell which which persuasive appeals Debbie used?

Directions	Copy
Shot #1	Picture this—you arrive home from a
Announcer	relaxing vacation. You expect to enter
	your house to find everything exactly as
	you left it, everything in its proper place.
	However, when you walk through your
	door, to your horror you find all of your
	possessions in shambles. The mattresses
	are slit open, and the television, CD player,
	VCR, and all of your jewelry are gone!
	You were robbed.

Shot #2	What you needed in your home, what you
Announcer	need in your home, in fact, what everyone
with alarm	needs in their homes, whether or not they
	have ever been victims of a robbery, is the
	Rambo Professional Alarm System. What
	the Rambo System does is get the burglar
	before the burglar gets you. The system's
	unique safety zone is activated whenever
	an intruder comes within a foot of your
	house. An alarm is set off, both within
	your house and at the nearest police
	station. It sounds like this. (BEEP)
	We are so sure that this system is effective
	that if it ever fails to function, we will give
	you double your money back.
Shot #3	Before you are unfortunate enough to be
Announcer	robbed, prevent the robbery. Get what
	America depends on—the Rambo
	Professional Alarm System. It's like having
	a one-person army protect your house.

Did Debbie's message appeal to a fear inside of you? Have you ever been robbed? Would you like total protection? What are the connotations of the name "Rambo"? What image does "Rambo" conjure up in your mind?

Students agreed that Debbie's message was effective because of its appeal to our need for security—particularly for a safe home. Even though the example in the message was about a robbery, the Rambo alarm system would protect individuals from all home invaders—including those who would inflict bodily harm. Of course, the name "Rambo" connotes a strong, brave protector—the part Sylvester Stallone played in the Rambo movies. The clever use of words, names and images is significant in moving people to action. Many product names have come from well-known stories, such as those of Greek and Roman mythology. For example, Atlas (tires), Ajax (detergent), Midas (mufflers) and Mercury (automobiles) were all names of mythological figures. They all have meanings related to the myths and to the functions of the products sold. These double meanings can have a persuasive effect.

UNDERSTANDING PERSUASIVE APPEALS

Emotional appeals and image-laden words are powerful persuaders. Because we often make decisions based on how we feel about things, as opposed to how we think through an argument rationally and logically, emotions play a large role in affecting our behavior. Aristotle, the Greek philosopher who lived from 384 to 322 B.C., identified three major types of persuasive appeals: *ethos, pathos,* and *logos.* These persuasive strategies have stood the test of time and are still used by speakers today.

Ethos can be defined as the personal appeal of the speaker. If your speech appears well organized and well prepared, and if you speak with confidence and conviction, you will demonstrate high ethos. If your ethos level is high, you and your message will become credible or believable.

Pathos consists of emotional appeals that play on how audience members feel about things. Appeals to guilt or patriotism are two examples of pathos often used in persuasive speeches. If you were giving a speech asking for donations to a charity, you might rely heavily on emotional appeals to create sympathy for those who need assistance.

Finally, *logos* depends on facts and evidence. When you research your topic and present solid facts and evidence to support your thesis, you are using a logical appeal. If your speech is packed with quotations, examples, illustrations, and statistics and you can give the sources for this verbal supporting material, your body of evidence will provide believable support for your major points.

Orations

Toward the end of your studies in speech, you may be asked to write and deliver an oration. An *oration* is a speech that combines emotional and logical appeals to prove that something is true or that a course of action should be taken. In preparing for an oration, you will go through the same kind of research process that you used to prepare an informative speech. However, this time you will think of your thesis statement a bit differently. It will become a persuasive proposition of fact, value, or policy. Instead of asking audience members to go out and do something (move to action) immediately after your speech, your purpose may be to affect their attitudes, or change how they feel about a problem or issue.

Persuasive propositions can be stated in one of three ways. The first type is a *proposition of fact* wherein you try to convince your audience that something is true or valid. "Arson is a major problem in the United States today" is a proposition of fact. To support a factual proposition, you will need to gather and present much specific evidence. Typically, the key verb in a factual proposition is some form of *to be, is,* or *are.*

In another type of persuasive proposition, you try to convince your audience of something's value; that it is good or bad, strong or weak, beneficial or detrimental, and so on. After evaluating a situation, you must persuade your audience that your judgment is correct. An example of a *proposition of value* is, "The Chicago Bulls is the finest team in professional basketball." Like a proposition of fact, you will need specific evidence to support your claim. Again, the key verb in this type of proposition is some form of *to be, is,* or *are.*

Finally, the third type of persuasive proposition is the *proposition of policy,* wherein you try to convince your audience that something should happen or should be done. An example of a proposition of policy is: "The legal driving age in our state should be raised to eighteen." Just as with the propositions of fact and value, you will need reasons and considerable concrete evidence to support your thesis. In this type of proposition, the key word is *should.*

Orations can be organized in a variety of ways. In the problem-solution approach, a problem is described, and then a solution is proposed. The cause-effect-solution paradigm describes the causes of the problem, details the effects, and poses the potential solution. No matter which type of organization you follow, all of the content must relate to your thesis or proposition. After each major point in your speech, you may want to provide summaries and transitions to relate your points back to your thesis in a clear, obvious way. The following oration outline for Bram's speech on frivolous lawsuits takes the cause-effect-solution form:

Topic: Frivolous lawsuits

Purpose: To convince the audience that frivolous lawsuits are a serious problem in our country today.

Introduction:

A forty-six-year-old gentleman stumbled out of a party in Chicago roaring drunk, his blood-alcohol level officially in the "stupor" classification at 0.341. On his way home, the man felt the urge to urinate and wandered onto the tracks of the Chicago transit line, past several signs that warned, "danger, keep out, and electric current." He climbed over a barrier and relieved himself onto the third rail, whereupon he was instantly electrocuted. His widow sued the Chicago Transit Authority and won a judgment of $1.5 million.[1] This is but one example of what has been happening in our court system over the past few years. We have experienced a litigation explosion with a huge increase in frivolous lawsuits. These lawsuits are clogging our court system and are making real justice for ordinary citizens like you and me difficult to obtain. *Frivolous lawsuits are a serious problem in our court systems today.*

I. The main cause of frivolous lawsuits is greedy people.

    A. Everyday citizens come up with "get rich quick" cases

        1. One greedy prisoner tried to sue five companies at once.

            a. He claimed that his yogurt had glass in it that cut his mouth; his conditioner burned his head; a can of shaving cream exploded in his face; a TV caught fire and burned his clothes; and his ibuprofin tablet caused him severe kidney damage.

            b. In each of the claims, he represented himself and called for hundreds of thousands of dollars in mental and physical damage.

            c. The judge handling his cases was so fed up with them that he had the prisoner's word processor taken away so that he couldn't use it to file any more lawsuits.

2. Many employees sue their employers
over various issues.

    a. The number of discrimination
lawsuits has risen 2,200 percent
over the past two decades.[2]

        1) People sue their employers by
saying that employers broke
one of the four laws that
prohibit discrimination
based on race, religion,
nationality, age or
disability.

        2) Of the cases fully
investigated by the
Equal Employment Opportunity
Commission, only 20 percent
had any merit.[3]

    b. Miami employment lawyer Michael
Casey says, "Before you fire
minorities, women, or anyone over
forty, or before you fail to hire

or promote them, you'd better have
your ducks lined up in a row ten
miles long."[4]

3. Some people have sued because their
violated "rights" included the right
to smoke, the right not to breathe
secondhand smoke, the right to teach
the use of condoms in schools, and the
right to keep students ignorant about
the use of condoms.[5]

4. In one of the most absurd cases,
Tom Morgan sued a fellow cashier for
"willfully and maliciously inflicting
severe mental stress and
humiliation by continually,
intentionally and repeatedly passing
gas directly at the plaintiff."[6]

B. Some lawyers search for and take on
frivolous cases.

1. In all-out litigation, defense costs
can range from $20,000 to $200,000
which can make taking on a lawsuit
quite profitable.[7]

2.   Of the 740,000 lawyers in the United
States, one-third are unemployed and
therefore may be willing to accept
frivolous cases.[8]

C.   Land developers can sue people who get in
the way of their developments.

    1.   Some land developers use SLAPPs
(Strategic Lawsuits
Against Public Participation)
to silence opponents of their
developments.

        a.   The League of Women Voters in
Beverly Hills, California, wrote
letters to newspapers criticizing
a proposed condominium development
and supporting a voter initiative
to stop it.

        b.   The developers then sued the
League for $63 million for libel,
slander, interference, and
conspiracy.[9]

    2.   People have SLAPPed back by suing
developers for harassment and misuse
of the court system.

     a.   One SLAPPing back case occurred
          when the J. G. Boswell Company
          sued three farmers over
          a newspaper advertisement that
          criticized the company's
          campaign.

     b.   The farmers sued the company back
          and won $13.5 million.[10]

[Transition] Now that you know some of the causes of frivolous lawsuits, let's take a look at some of the dangerous effects they are having.

II. Frivolous lawsuits have had negative effects for both businesses and individuals.

    A.   Frivolous lawsuits are destroying small businesses and jobs.

        1.   One small winery was sued, along with the industry's giants, by a group of lawyers saying that the wineries were endangering public health by using lead foils on bottles.[11]

        2.   Although the wineries won the case, they had to pay $456,000 in legal fees or face an appeal.[12]

        3.   Victor Monia was working to improve
            the quality of life in his town by
            halting a local development when he
            was SLAPPed.

        4.   He became so involved in fighting the
            case that he lost his job.[13]

   B.   Frivolous lawsuits are clogging our court
      system.

        1.   Every case that is filed takes a
            considerable amount of time and
            expense to process, and the huge
            number of lawsuits, makes the court
            system sluggish.

        2.   As frivolous lawsuits clog the courts,
            important suits are slowed down
            causing people to drop them because it
            takes too long and costs too much to
            pursue real justice.

[Transition] These dangerous effects can be stopped
if we put an end to the excess filing
of frivolous lawsuits. Here are a few ways to
do just that.

III. Laws and regulations can be implemented to cut
     down the number of frivolous lawsuits.

   A.   One rule aimed at stopping frivolous
      lawsuits is the controversial Rule 11.

1. Rule 11 requires judges to impose penalties on lawyers who file frivolous lawsuits.[14]

2. Rule 11 is said to be just as important to our justice system as the Geneva Convention is to war; it is an attempt to restrain the worst atrocities that a barbaric institution visits upon its hostages.[15]

B. England provides a model of how to deter frivolous lawsuits.

1. One difference between the U.S. and British legal systems is that in England juries are only used in criminal trials, thereby decreasing the number of large jury awards.

2. In England, the attorney's fees of both the winning and losing parties are paid by the losing party; therefore, an innocent person can fight a case and win without going bankrupt from legal fees.[16]

3. British courts allow little pretrial discovery, which speeds up the legal process and saves time and money.

C. In medical malpractice cases, some states
    require a signed affidavit by another
    medical professional in the same field to
    ensure a case's legitimacy.[17]

    1. The second professional reviews the
        case to see if it has legal merit.

    2. The purpose of this affidavit is to
        reduce the number of frivolous medical
        malpractice suits and to do so before
        they take up time in courts.[18]

    3. Although this idea just applies to the
        medical field, it can be copied and
        used in other fields.

Conclusion:

   Christopher Duffy stole a car from a parking
lot and was killed in an accident while he was
driving that stolen car. The estate of car thief
Duffy subsequently sued the proprietor of the
parking lot for failing to prevent auto theft.[20]
Cases such as this one are clogging our court
system. People who are just looking to make a quick
buck through frivolous lawsuits must be stopped
before the litigation explosion becomes a bomb that
destroys our system of justice.

ENDNOTES

1. John Berendt, "The Lawsuit," <u>Esquire</u>,
    May 1993, 37.

2. Jay Finegan, "Law and Disorder," <u>INC.</u>,
    April, 1994, 64.

3. Finegan, 67.

4. Finegan, 66.

5. Jesse Birnbaum, "Crybabies: Eternal Victims,"
    <u>Time</u>, August 12, 1991, 17.

6. Birnbaum, 17.

7. Finegan, 68.

8. Finegan, 68.

9. Robert H. Boyle, "Activists at Risk of
    Being SLAPPed," <u>Sports Illustrated,</u>
    March 25, 1991, 9.

10. Boyle, 9.

11. Martha Culbertson, "Grapes of Wrath," <u>Newsweek</u>,
    May 16, 1994, 10.

12. Culbertson, 10.

13. Boyle, 11.

14. David Frum, "Shoot the Hostages," <u>Forbes</u>,
    December 21, 1992, 138.

15. Frum, 138.

16. Rodney Gould, "Agency Liability," <u>Weekly</u>, March 21, 1991, 14.

17. Wilton F. Lunch, "Taking Aim at Frivolous Lawsuits," <u>Building Design & Construction</u>, October 1992, 31.

18. Lunch, 31.

19. Birnbaum, 17.

WORKS CITED

Berendt, John. "The Lawsuit." <u>Esquire,</u> May 1993, 37.

Birnbaum, Jesse. "Crybabies: Eternal Victims." <u>Time</u>, August 12, 1991, 16-19.

Boyle, Robert H. "Activists at Risk of Being SLAPPed." <u>Sports Illustrated</u>, March 25, 1991, 9-12..

Culbertson, Martha. "Grapes of Wrath." <u>Newsweek</u>, May 16, 1994, 10.

"Don't Trample Prisoners' Rights." <u>The New York Times</u>, March 27, 1994, E16.

Finegan, Jay. "Law and Disorder," <u>INC.</u>, April, 1994, 64-68.

Frum, David. "Shoot the Hostages." <u>Forbes</u>,
December 21, 1992, 138.

Fulton William, and Morris Newman. "SLAPPing Back."
<u>California Business</u>, March 1991, 22.

Gould, Rodney. "Agency Liability." <u>Weekly</u>,
March 21, 1991, 14.

"Investor Suits Talk of Town." <u>The New York Times</u>,
March 24, 1994, C5.

Lunch, Milton F. "Taking Aim at Frivolous
Lawsuits." <u>Building Design and Construction</u>,
October 1992, 31.

Pollock, Ellen John. "Copy-cat Fines Affirmed."
<u>The Wall Street Journal</u>, May 5, 1994, B2.

Shapiro, Bruce. "Hard Case." <u>The Nation</u>,
December 7, 1992, 688.

Souter, Gavin. "Excess Litigation Ailing
European Countries," <u>Business Insurance</u>,
May 10, 1993, 28.

Tabor, Mary B. W., "Suit Filer's Word Processor
Loses Out in Court." <u>The New York Times</u>,
March 29, 1994, A116.

The preceding speech contained a wealth of factual and anecdotal (real stories) information to convince the audience that frivolous lawsuits are indeed a problem. By combining logos, ethos, and pathos, Bram could truly persuade his audience to think seriously about this problem. Can you pick out the emotional appeals in this speech? Would any of the content make you angry? How could the information in this speech affect you personally?

SELECTING AN ORATION TOPIC

Listed below in the form of propositions of fact, value, or policy are several possible topics. Because these propositions are controversial and have a wealth of information available on them, they make viable oration topics.

1. Euthanasia (mercy killing) should be legal.
2. Vegetarianism is more nourishing than a normal diet.
3. Handgun possession should be outlawed.
4. Too much emphasis is placed on SAT/ACT scores for college admission.
5. The government should allocate more money to encourage development of the arts.
6. Teenage runaways are a growing problem.

7. Welfare practices should be altered to encourage independence.
8. Medical quackery is widely practiced in the U.S. today.
9. Gasoline taxes should be increased to help support public transportation.
10. Journalists should have the right to maintain and protect confidential sources.

Conclusion

You are now ready to put all the skills covered in this book to good use. Analyze your audience; choose a topic of interest to both you and your audience; gather and organize your information; relate your content to your thesis; combine emotional and logical appeals; use both nonverbal and vocal aspects of delivery in an enthusiastic and purposeful manner. You can do it. You are now ready to give an excellent speech. Good luck!

Bibliography

Ahrens, Art, and Eddie Gold. *Day by Day in Chicago Cubs History*. New York: Leisure Press, 1982.

Birnbaum, Jesse. "Crybabies: Eternal Victims" *Time*. August 12, 1991, 16.

Ellis, Rosemary. "Skin Cancer" *The Press*. June 15, 1990, 61.

Elson, E. F. and Alberta Peck. *The Art of Speaking*. Boston, MA: Ginn and Company, 1966.

Jeroski, Sharon, David Fisher, Patricia McIntosh, and Helen Zwick. *Speak for Yourself*. Evanston, IL: McDougal, Littell and Co. 1990.

Kramer, Rita. *Ed School Follies*. New York: The Free Press, 1991.

McCutcheon, Randall, James Schaffer and Joseph Wycoff. *Communication Matters*. St. Paul, MN: West Publishing Company, 1994.

Prentice, Diana and James Payne. *Public Speaking Today!* Lincolnwood, IL: National Textbook Company, 1989.

Wallechinsky, David, Irving Wallace and Amy Wallace. *The Book of Lists*. New York: Bantam Books, 1978.